3-45

£ 2.20www

Critical Guides to Spanish Texts

Critical Guides to Spanish Texts

EDITED BY J.E. VAREY AND A.D. DEYERMOND

LOPE DE VEGA

Fuenteovejuna

J.B. Hall

Senior Lecturer in Spanish
University College, Swansea

Grant & Cutler Ltd *in association with*
Tamesis Books Ltd 1985

© Grant & Cutler Ltd
1985
ISBN 0 7293 0223 7

I.S.B.N. 84-599-0681-7

DEPÓSITO LEGAL: V. 951 - 1985

Printed in Spain by
Artes Gráficas Soler, S.A., Valencia
for
GRANT & CUTLER LTD
11 BUCKINGHAM STREET, LONDON, W.C.2

Contents

Preface

References to the text of Lope's *Fuenteovejuna* are to Francisco López Estrada's edition (which includes the *Fuenteovejuna* of Cristóbal de Monroy), *Fuente Ovejuna (Dos comedias)*, Clásicos Castalia, 10 (Madrid: Castalia, 1969). Works given in the Bibliographical Note are referred to by an italic number, followed as required by a page-reference, e.g. (*3*, pp.29-30).

I should like to record my gratitude to the Editors, Professor J.E. Varey and Professor A.D. Deyermond, for their helpful comments on my original typescript and for their unfailing encouragement and patience during the preparation of this study.

Sketty, Swansea
1983

Introduction

'Twixt kings and tyrants there's this difference known,
Kings seek their subjects' good; tyrants their own.
(Robert Herrick, 1591-1674)

A small-scale popular revolt in an obscure village, a minor incident in an unsettled period of Spanish history, the affair of Fuenteovejuna might ordinarily have been quickly forgotten, even though it did involve the killing of an important nobleman, a Comendador in a chivalric order. That it is still remembered over five centuries later is due to two things: firstly, the determination of the villagers who refused, even under torture, to denounce the ringleaders to the authorities investigating the incident, so that 'Fuenteovejuna lo hizo' became a proverbial affirmation of defiance and solidarity; secondly, because in the early seventeenth century Spain's leading dramatist based upon the story one of his best plays. Lope's *Fuenteovejuna* is an exciting drama of love, honour and loyalty in which a local uprising acquires national significance: the Comendador who tyrannizes the villagers is also a prominent rebel against the Crown, so that the villagers and their sovereigns are opposed to a common enemy. We cannot tell how successful the play was in its own time; a later dramatist, Cristóbal de Monroy (1612-49), also wrote a *Fuenteovejuna*, which might suggest that Lope's version was sufficiently popular to justify a second treatment of the story, but this is mere speculation.[1]

Like other Golden Age dramas, *Fuenteovejuna* was not acceptable to the neo-classical tastes of the eighteenth century, but the nineteenth century showed a gradual revival of interest: the play was translated into French (1822) and German (1845), and published in the Biblioteca de Autores Españoles in 1857. Serious critical interest in *Fuenteovejuna* began with Menéndez

[1] For a useful study of Monroy's play and a comparison of it with Lope's *Fuenteovejuna*, see *3*, pp.181-94 and 347-59.

y Pelayo's edition and study of 1899 (*26*). He saw the play as pro-monarchic but as having extremely strong democratic implications as well, and productions in modern times have tended to politicize the play and to see it in radical or revolutionary terms; this was the case with an early production in Tsarist Russia (1876), and *Fuenteovejuna* has been very popular in the Soviet Union since 1919, in a version which omits the Reyes Católicos and concentrates on the villagers' heroic struggle against an aristocratic tyrant. Productions in other countries have often modified the play along similar lines: Lorca's version, performed by La Barraca in the 1930s, had the Comendador dressed as a village *cacique*, and the Reyes, though apparently not vanishing altogether, seem to have been left out of the concluding scenes. Such progressive approaches to *Fuenteovejuna* were countered during the Civil War by attempts to claim the play for the extreme Right, with the revolt of the villagers being likened to the Nationalist uprising against the Republic in July, 1936. A number of more recent productions have sought to impress by emphasizing and adding to the elements of sadism and of sexual depravity found in the play.[2]

A more honest approach to *Fuenteovejuna* is to respect the text and to illustrate its dramatic and poetic qualities and clarify its meaning by detailed analysis while setting the play in the context of the theatrical conventions of its age as regards both technique and themes. Such an approach may show that *Fuenteovejuna* has certain enduring artistic and thematic characteristics which can be readily enjoyed and accepted in our own time, while others can be appreciated and understood by whoever has the sympathy and imagination needed to view them historically. This has been the aim of the many studies of the play which have appeared in the last few decades, and it is also the aim of the present work.

[2] For a fuller account of translations, adaptations and productions in modern times, see *17*.

1 *Date and Sources*

Lope's *Fuenteovejuna* was first published in the *Docena parte de las comedias de Lope de Vega* (Madrid, 1619); the dates of the play's composition and first performance are unknown, although Morley and Bruerton concluded from a study of the metre that it was written no earlier than 1611 and no later than 1618, most probably between 1612 and 1614.[3]

Lope based his play upon supposedly historical events: in 1476 the villagers of Fuenteovejuna[4] in the province of Córdoba rose up against their lord, Fernán Gómez de Guzmán, a Comendador of the chivalric Order of Calatrava; Fernán was murdered by the rebels, allegedly on account of the brutal treatment which he had inflicted on the community over a long period. When the royal authorities arrived to investigate the incident, all the villagers, even when tortured, refused to say more than 'Fuenteovejuna lo hizo', with the result that no individual culprit for the killing could be identified, and nobody was eventually put on trial.

The incident was still remembered in Lope's time, and the stand taken by the people of Fuenteovejuna was looked upon — not always with approval — as a proverbial instance of

[3] Two impressions of the *Docena parte* appeared in 1619; there are some not very significant differences between their versions of the text of *Fuenteovejuna*. For these see e.g. *3*, pp.29-30; *4*, pp.67-70; *5*, pp.xliv-xlviii; and the review of *3* by Victor Dixon, *Bulletin of Hispanic Studies*, 48 (1971), 330-31. For the date of composition, see S. Griswold Morley and C. Bruerton, *Cronología de las comedias de Lope de Vega* (Madrid: Gredos, 1968), pp.330-31. J. Robles Pazos ('Sobre la fecha de *Fuenteovejuna*', *Modern Language Notes*, 50 (1935), 179-82) maintained that *Fuenteovejuna* could be no later than 1613 and was probably written during that year. He based his argument on the fact that Tirso de Molina's *La Santa Juana* (late 1613 or early 1614) has a number of parallels with *Fuenteovejuna*, of which it might be an imitation. However, as Morley suggested, Tirso could equally well have influenced Lope ('*Fuente Ovejuna* and its Theme-Parallels', *Hispanic Review*, 4 (1936), 303-11).

[4] Properly Fuente*abe*juna, a place famous for its bees and honey. The corrupt form Fuente*ove*juna (usually rendered by English translators as Sheep-Well — cf. Laurencia's remarks on the timidity of the men, ll.1758-59) — seems to have become established very early. See *3*, pp.13-14, n.14.

solidarity. For instance, according to the records of the Cabildo or town council of Tunja, on 27 August 1594 a group of citizens made an attempt to support collectively a motion on which only one should have voted, thereby eliciting from the president (as he tore up the paper with their names) the irritated remark that 'no se había de votar como en Fuenteovejuna, coadunándose'.[5] In a Lenten sermon published in 1609, Fr Juan de Luna, retelling Christ's parable of the tenants who kill the vineyard owner's son in order to keep the property themselves, makes the murderers agree to say only 'todos, Fuenteovejuna' when asked who committed the crime.[6] In his *Emblemas morales* of 1610, Sebastián de Covarrubias Horozco refers to the uprising and the failure to identify those responsible for the Comendador's death, and seems to assume that his readers will be familiar with the story:

> Grande es la confusión de un juez cristiano
> cuando en un caso atroz Fuenteovejuna
> con atrevida y vengativa mano,
> sin Dios, sin Rey, sin ley, toda se aúna
> de hecho a un hecho bárbaro, inhumano
> sin que se halle claridad ninguna
> cuál sea el culpado, cuál el inocente
> en la comunidad de tanta gente.[7]

Covarrubias's sympathies clearly lie here with the thwarted judge who must let criminals go free rather than commit the injustice of punishing the innocent along with the guilty. However, he appears less prejudiced against the villagers when in his *Tesoro de la lengua castellana* (1611) he explains the origin of 'Fuente Ovejuna lo hizo', a 'proverbio trillado' used of cases

[5] Cited by Miguel Aguilera, 'Membranza de Fuenteovejuna en el cabildo Tunjano', *Repertorio Boyacense*, 51 (1965), 2219-29, at p.2228. See also *15*, p.46.

[6] Juan de Luna, *Sermones de Quaresma, desde la Septuagésima hasta la mañana de la Resurrección* (Madrid, 1609), pp.244-45.

[7] Sebastián de Covarrubias Horozco, *Emblemas morales* (Madrid, 1610), fol.297, emblem 97.

in which no single person can be found guilty of a crime in which several participated:

> ...en el año de mil y quatrocientos y setenta y seis, en el qual se dio la batalla de Toro, como toda Castilla estuviesse revuelta en parcialidades, los de Fuente Ovejuna, una noche del mes de abril, se apellidaron para dar la muerte a Hernán Pérez [*sic*] de Guzmán, Comendador mayor de Calatrava, por los muchos agravios que pretendían averles hecho. Y entrando en su misma casa le mataron a pedradas, y aunque sobre el caso fueron embiados juezes pesquisidores, que atormentaron a muchos dellos, assí hombres como mugeres, no les pudieron sacar otra palabra más désta: 'Fuente Ovejuna lo hizo'; de do quedó el proverbio quando el delito es notorio, y en particular no hallan quién lo aya hecho siendo muchos los delincuentes, dezir 'Fuente Ovejuna lo hizo'.[8]

Covarrubias seems to have reservations about the extent of the abuses which the villagers claimed to have suffered from the Comendador ('los muchos agravios que *pretendían* averles hecho'); his reference to all of Castile being 'revuelta en parcialidades' may imply that he suspected the villagers of craftily hoping that their killing of Fernán Gómez might pass if not unnoticed, then perhaps at least unpunished, in the general civil unrest; nonetheless, his tone is noticeably more moderate here than in the *Emblemas morales*.

It is debatable whether Lope was inspired to write a play on Fuenteovejuna by reading Covarrubias; Moir has argued strongly (*27*) that the *Emblemas morales* were a crucial influence and that certain passages in the play are inspired by various emblems in the collection, but his conclusions have not met with universal acceptance (see *5*, p.xi, n.6). Lope's view of the uprising as morally justified though legally incorrect has little in common with Covarrubias's denunciation of it in the *Emblemas*

---

[8] Sebastián de Covarrubias Horozco, *Tesoro de la lengua castellana o española* (Madrid, 1611), fol.416v.

morales — Esteban, for instance, applies such epithets as 'bárbaro' and 'inhumano' to the Comendador and his henchmen (l.1701) — but it would be rash to assume that Lope was therefore deliberately setting out to provide a corrective. It seems best to conclude that although Covarrubias might have given Lope the idea for his play this is by no means certain. Lope could equally well have realized on his own that a story so violent and controversial was obviously rich in dramatic potential and was sufficiently well known to attract audiences to a play based upon it.

Lope's principal source of information on the revolt of the villagers was clearly the *Chrónica de las tres Ordenes y Cavallerías de Santiago, Calatrava y Alcántara* (Toledo, 1572) by Fray Francisco de Rades y Andrada, a royal chaplain and himself a member of the Order of Calatrava.[9] According to Rades (ff. 79v-80v), Fernán Gómez was a supporter of Afonso V of Portugal, a pretender to the throne of Castile;[10] he billeted soldiers loyal to the pretender's faction upon the people of Fuenteovejuna: 'y consentía que aquella gente hiziesse grandes agravios y deshonrras a los de Fuenteovejuna, sobre comérseles sus haziendas.' The Comendador himself was guilty of robbing and offending the villagers:

...avía hecho grandes agravios y deshonrras a los de la villa, tomándoles por fuerza sus hijas y mugeres, y robándoles sus haziendas para sustentar aquellos soldados que tenía, con título y color que el Maestre don Rodrigo Téllez Girón su señor lo mandava, porque entonces seguía aquel partido del Rey de Portogal.

As a result of such ill-treatment the villagers unanimously

[9] Kirschner (*15*, p.55) suggests that Rades was the source for the details of the affair which Covarrubias gives, and also inspired the brief reference to it made by Juan de Mariana in Bk 24, ch.11 of his *Historia general de España* (Toledo, 1601). Rades's account of the uprising is reproduced by Menéndez Pelayo (*26*, pp.172-74).

[10] On the death of Enrique IV of Castile in 1474, Afonso's wife Juana claimed that she, not Isabel, was the rightful heir to the throne (see *Fuenteovejuna*, ll.90-103). There is a useful account of the conflict in J.H. Elliott, *Imperial Spain, 1469-1716* (London: Edward Arnold, 1963), pp.5-12.

resolved — 'todos de un consentimiento y voluntad' — to attack
and kill the Comendador; Rades mentions that they were led by
their local officials, the 'Alcaldes, Regidores, Justicia y
Regimiento', and that they chanted such slogans as 'vivan los
Reyes don Fernando y doña Isabel, y mueran los traydores y
malos christianos'; the implication appears to be that they were
moved by a patriotic sense of loyalty to the Reyes Católicos as
well as by a wish to take vengeance for their purely local
grievances. Although Rades does seem to sympathize with the
villagers he does not play down the violence of their actions: he
describes their refusal to accept the Comendador's offers to
make restitution to those whom he had offended, their killing of
fourteen of his men and the 'furor maldito y ravioso' with which
they finally murdered him, throwing him alive from a window
on to the swords and spears of those below:

> Después de caýdo en tierra, le arrancaron las barbas con
> grande crueldad; y otros con los pomos de las espadas le
> quebraron las dientes. A todo esto añadieron palabras feas
> y descorteses, y grandes injurias contra el Comendador
> mayor, y contra su padre y madre.

There follows an account of how the village women came to
rejoice at the Comendador's death, parading under a banner
which they had made specially, and led by their own officers:
'avían hecho para esto una vandera, y nombrado Capitana y
Alférez.' By the time Rades has described the villagers'
mutilation of the body, their refusal to permit Christian burial
and their plundering of the Comendador's house, the reader
may well have begun to feel some sympathy for Fernán Gómez,
despite the villainies attributed to him:

> ...llevaron el cuerpo con gran regocijo a la plaza; y allí
> todos, hombres y mugeres le hizieron pedazos, arras-
> trándole y haziendo en él grandes crueldades y escarnios; y
> no quisieron darle a sus criados para enterrarle. Demás
> desto dieron sacomano a su casa, y le robaron toda su
> hazienda.

A more favourable impression of the villagers is given by their
steadfast refusal to denounce the instigators or ringleaders of the
revolt when questioned by the Juez Pesquisidor sent by
Fernando and Isabel:

> Preguntávales el Juez: '¿quién mató al Comendador
> mayor?' Respondían ellos: 'Fuente-ovejuna.' Pregun-
> távales: '¿quién es Fuente-ovejuna?' Respondían: 'todos
> los vezinos desta villa...' Y lo que más es de admirar es que
> el Juez hizo dar tormento a muchas mugeres y mancebos
> de poca edad, y tuvieron la misma constancia y ánimo que
> los varones muy fuertes.

Finally, according to Rades, the judge gave the Reyes Católicos
an account of the affair, 'y sus Altezas siendo informadas de las
tyranías del Comendador mayor, por las quales avía merescido
la muerte, mandaron que se quedasse el negocio sin más
averiguación.' Rades does not say that the impossibility of
identifying the ringleaders was a factor in the decision to
abandon the investigation, but this might reasonably be
inferred; as has been seen, the belief became an essential element
in the popular versions of the story, and in Lope's play the king,
after learning of the Comendador's misdeeds (from the
villagers, not the judge), remarks:

> Pues no puede averiguarse
> el suceso por escrito,
> aunque fue grave el delito,
> por fuerza ha de perdonarse. (ll.2442-45)

The accuracy of Rades's version of the uprising was
questioned by Aníbal (6) who alleged that it was grossly unfair
to the Comendador, and drew attention to the far more
favourable impression of him given by the fifteenth-century
chronicler Alfonso de Palencia (1423-92).[11] Palencia presents
the Comendador (whom he calls Fernando Ramírez de Guzmán)

[11] *Crónica de Enrique IV*, trans. A. Paz y Melia, IV, Colección de Escritores
Castellanos, 134 (Madrid, 1908), pp.199-203.

as a loyal supporter of the Reyes Católicos and an opponent of the Maestre of Calatrava, Rodrigo Téllez Girón; the latter, with other partisans of the Portuguese pretender, secretly incited the people of Fuenteovejuna to turn against their lord, the pretext being an increase in the taxes which he levied upon them. This, Palencia claims, was the sole complaint that they could have had, since the Comendador had always treated them well; in fact he was so respected that after his death the murderers were obliged to accuse him falsely of immoral conduct in order to justify his killing. Palencia makes no mention of the judge's investigation or of the villagers' courageous silence under torture, and concludes his account by saying that the Reyes Católicos failed to punish anyone simply because of their preoccupation with more pressing matters arising out of the civil conflicts of the period. Aníbal maintained that Palencia was apparently giving the true version of the Fuenteovejuna story, that Lope was ignorant of it, that he followed Rades in making the Comendador a 'wenching villain' and thus unwittingly committed an injustice which 'stained for all time the character of one of the noblest men of this lurid epoch' (*6*, p.718).

More reprehensible, because quite deliberate, was for Aníbal the way in which Lope had given Fernán Gómez a completely unhistorical role in the secondary or background plot of his play. This concerns the capture of Ciudad Real by the forces of the Maestre of Calatrava, and the subsequent retaking of the town by the army of Fernando and Isabel, to whom the Maestre finally submits, and by whom he is pardoned on account of his youth and his assurances of future loyalty. Immediately before his account of the Fuenteovejuna incident Rades gives a description of the Ciudad Real campaign (ff. 78v-79r). Lope follows this closely but makes one very important change: Rades tells us that it was the Maestre's brother and cousin who induced him to support Afonso of Portugal and make war on Fernando and Isabel, but Lope makes Fernán Gómez the instigator of the attack on Ciudad Real, and presents him and the Maestre as joint commanders of the Calatravan army; the two plots of *Fuenteovejuna* thus have a common villain. Lope may have been given the idea of linking them in this way by Rades's remarks

that Fernán Gómez was a supporter of the pretender, and that
the villagers accused him of treachery to the Reyes Católicos; his
unprincipled attempt to blame the Maestre for his requisitioning
of the villagers' goods ('robándoles sus haziendas...con título y
color que el Maestre don Rodrigo Téllez Girón su señor lo
mandava') has been developed by Lope into an unscrupulous
exploitation of the young man for the furtherance of the
Comendador's political schemes.

Aníbal was of course right to say that by making the
Comendador the villain of the Ciudad Real episode as well as
that of the Fuenteovejuna episode, Lope was 'wilfully and
purposely' tampering with historical fact (*6*, p.691). However,
this is as irrelevant for an appreciation and understanding of the
play as the truth about the real circumstances of the villagers'
revolt.[12] Lope was after all writing a drama, not history, and his
criteria were those of aesthetic and moral effectiveness rather
than of historical accuracy. By bringing in the Ciudad Real
affair he gives his play variety through the addition of a
secondary plot of national as opposed to local and individual
significance; by making Fernán Gómez the villain of this
secondary plot Lope gives a fuller picture of him as a man who
upsets the idyllic rural harmony of Fuenteovejuna through his
cruelty, greed and lust, as well as menacing the unity and
stability of the state through his political ambitions. If Lope
knew Palencia's account of the Fuenteovejuna uprising (and it is
quite conceivable that he did), then he consciously rejected it in
favour of Rades; the latter's version suited his purposes better,
according with Golden Age views on the moral superiority of
rural life (*aldea*) over that of the town and the court (*corte*), and
offering through the death of Fernán Gómez a striking example
of that sense of poetic justice which is so important in Golden

[12] Discussing the contemporary documents on the uprising which Ramírez de
Arellano published in 1901 (*30*), Salomon notes that the leaders included
merchants, clerks and artisans but not a single peasant. He concludes that the
revolt was undeniably an urban and in some ways a bourgeois affair, apparently
instigated by the citizens of Córdoba, eager to reduce the influence of the
Calatravans (*32*, pp.825-26). Rades remarks that after killing the Comendador
the villagers sought the protection of the City of Córdoba. Lope has Fernando
put the village under his own protection (ll.2446-49).

Age drama.[13]

For Lope and his contemporaries artistic originality lay more in the manner than the matter: in an era that tended to be intellectually conservative and had comparatively little sense of the possibility of progress, the artist was not expected to break new ground in terms of plot or ideas so much as to present what was familiar in a new and pleasing fashion — 'dezir nueva y ornadamente las cosas comunes', as Fernando de Herrera put it.[14] The artist worked within an established tradition which he developed and modified, and his work was in many ways a variation on a theme. The process of artistic creation began with *invención*: this had nothing to do with our modern term 'invention' as implying something wholly new, but meant (as its etymology suggests) finding or 'coming upon' something already extant as a basis for one's work[15] — in the present case the chronicle of Rades y Andrada. Having found his raw materials, the artist could then embark on the second stage of the process: *disposición*, making them his own by modifying, reshaping and rearranging them. Lope's originality in *Fuenteovejuna* lies less in the story (which comes essentially from Rades) or in the themes (which embody the received wisdom of the age) than in the play's structure, characterization and style. The end result is a work of art on the one hand lively, fast-moving and exciting, and on the other rich in ideas, mentally stimulating and morally profitable. *Fuenteovejuna* thus fulfils the great demand of the time: that art should combine *deleite* with *doctrina*, as the Golden Age rendered the Horatian concepts of *dulce* and *utile*.

[13] Although Palencia's chronicle was not published until early in this century, manuscript copies of the Latin original and of a Castilian version by an unknown translator were quite widely available in the Golden Age. On poetic justice see for example A.A. Parker, *The Approach to the Spanish Drama of the Golden Age*, Diamante Series, 6 (London: The Hispanic and Luso-Brazilian Councils, 1957). A revised and expanded version of this essay, entitled 'The Spanish Drama of the Golden Age: A Method of Analysis and Interpretation', is to be found in *The Great Playwrights: twenty-five plays with commentaries by critics and scholars chosen and introduced by Eric Bentley* (New York: Doubleday, 1970), I, pp.679-707.

[14] *Obras de Garci Lasso de la Vega con anotaciones de Fernando de Herrera* (Seville, 1580), p.292.

[15] The corresponding verb is *hallar*.

2 *Staging*

The kind of public theatre for which *Fuenteovejuna* was written had its origins in town squares, innyards or the patios of private houses hired out for the purpose of theatrical performance. When, from about the middle of the sixteenth century, permanent purpose-built theatres were constructed, they kept to the familiar hollow-square pattern and were commonly known as *corrales*.[16] By the early seventeenth century the theatre was the most popular form of entertainment in Madrid. Audiences were drawn from all social classes, and included women and members of the clergy, for with its standard fare of theologically orthodox and pro-monarchic dramas (known as *comedias*) the theatre was generally considered respectable, despite the often scandalous lives led by actors, actresses and dramatists, such as Lope himself.

The main acting-space in the *corral* theatre was an apron stage protruding into the audience, with a door on each side at the back for exits and entrances. Between the doors and usually concealed by a curtain was a recess which formed an inner stage or discovery space. This is used twice in *Fuenteovejuna*, firstly at the end of Act I when Frondoso hides from the Comendador (l.778), and then in Act II when he and Laurencia playfully hide from her father and uncle (l.1316).[17] Above was the upper stage, a balcony which ran round the other three sides of the theatre, accommodating some of the audience. The upper stage might represent a hill-top, the walls of a castle or city, or the upper storey of a house; however, its use does not seem to be called for in *Fuenteovejuna*; although in Act II we see the Maestre and

[16] For a full description of the theatres of Golden Age Spain see N.D. Shergold, *A History of the Spanish Stage from Medieval Times until the End of the Seventeenth Century* (Oxford: Clarendon Press, 1967).

[17] Alternatively they might hide behind one of the uprights supporting the balcony or upper stage.

Comendador lamenting the fall of Ciudad Real to the royal army, it is plain (ll.1460-62) that they are not on the ramparts but observing the final stages of the battle from a distance as they prepare to escape.

The kind of sets and scenery possible in the proscenium-arch type of theatre (which was to appear in Spain later in the seventeenth century) could not be achieved in a *corral*. The location of scenes is consequently often left vague and has no special significance: thus the play opens at the residence of the Maestre, although the town (presumably Calatrava — see l.1465) is not named and is referred to simply as 'la villa' (ll.2, 44). The appearance of the king and queen makes it plain that we are now at one of the royal palaces (ll.635, 1920), but the audience is not told where; in Act III one of the villagers says that Fernando and Isabel are going to Córdoba (l.1677), and it is presumably there or nearby that they receive the Maestre, the judge and the people of Fuenteovejuna at the end of the Act (ll.2290-453), but this can only be inferred. On other occasions it is more important for the audience to know where a particular scene is taking place, and so after the opening at the Maestre's residence we are informed that the action has shifted to Fuenteovejuna (ll.177-78); likewise at the end of Act I, following a scene at the court of the Reyes Católicos, Laurencia's words to Frondoso (ll.723-26) indicate that they are near the stream outside the village. Act II begins in the village square, and the audience must be told (ll.1139-40) when the scene changes to the open country some way off, where Mengo and Jacinta will be unable to find help when the Comendador and his men come upon them. The action then returns to the village where Frondoso has dared to show himself, having seen Fernán Gómez ride away (ll.1277-84). In Act III a remark by the Comendador (ll.1856-57) indicates that after the initial scene in the council chamber we are now at his house.[18]

Stage properties were simple: *Fuenteovejuna* requires weapons such as swords for the Comendador and his followers, and arms, some improvised, for the villagers when they attack him; Fernán Gómez has a crossbow which Frondoso seizes and

[18] On the question of scene locations see *8*.

carries off at the end of Act I; Mengo, the shepherd, needs a
sling with which he tries to defend Jacinta and with which the
Comendador's men bind his hands before he is flogged (ll.1234-
35); Esteban, the *alcalde*, carries his *vara* or staff of office which
Fernán Gómez snatches in order to beat him (ll.1631-34); in the
final act a dummy head of Fernán Gómez is brought in on a
spear and in an effective piece of visual symbolism Esteban
orders it to be taken away as Juan Rojo enters with a shield
bearing the royal coat of arms (l.2069). The only items of
furniture likely to be necessary are chairs for the king and queen
in the court scenes, and seats or benches, possibly for the
meeting of the village council at the start of Act III and certainly
for the opening of Act II when some of the men of
Fuenteovejuna are talking together in the square (they politely
stand when the Comendador enters and he, with false cordiality,
orders them to remain seated, ll.940-48). The villagers' tribute of
food and drink for the Comendador, which Esteban describes in
such detail (ll.549-78), would probably not be brought out on
stage.

The costumes of the aristocratic characters would be lavish,
especially those of the king and queen; the Maestre and
Comendador would also be richly attired, as the description
given by Flores (ll.469-96) suggests. There is a certain amount of
visual symbolism in the costumes: the Comendador wears
embroidered on his doublet the emblem of his order, a red cross
standing for the Christian and chivalric ideals which he professes
and betrays, and of which Laurencia forcefully reminds him
(ll.810-13). Save for the wedding at the end of Act II, when
presumably they appear in appropriate rustic finery, the
villagers wear plain everyday dress suited to the simple, moral
lives they lead — Laurencia, significantly, refuses the elegant
costume with which the Comendador's men tempt her to
become his mistress (ll.198-209). Her dishevelled appearance
after escaping from the Comendador's house in Act III gives the
impression that she has been raped (see ll.1750-52), and it is only
at the end of the play that we learn that this was not in fact so
(ll.2402-13).

Given the limitations of the *corral* theatre, one can readily appreciate why Lope and his school wrote as they did: their socially mixed and proverbially impatient audiences could not be diverted by any visual spectacle involving elaborate sets or effects such as transformation scenes achieved through the use of stage machinery.[19] Instead they were offered lively and fast-moving entertainment, frequently based on a straightforward confrontation between good and evil. In *Fuenteovejuna* such a confrontation is expressed through the conflict of loyalty and treachery, love and lust, order and disorder, honour and dishonour, 'los casos de la honra', as Lope himself remarked, being very popular with Spaniards of all classes.[20] The level of emotional intensity is kept high throughout most Golden Age *comedias*, with many stirring or poignant passages offering good scope for the actors' histrionic skills: examples in *Fuenteovejuna* would include the Comendador's speech persuading the Maestre to rebel (ll.69-140), the accounts by Flores of the capture of Ciudad Real (ll.455-528) and of the death of Fernán Gómez (ll.1948-2013), Laurencia's description of her escape and her demand for action to save Frondoso's life (ll.1723-93), her later soliloquy in sonnet form describing her fears for his safety after the Comendador's death (ll.2161-74), and the repentant Maestre's plea for forgiveness from Fernando and Isabel (ll.2310-37).

Light relief is provided by the clown or *gracioso*, usually a comic servant or peasant; Mengo, though he has his serious side, fulfils this role in *Fuenteovejuna*.[21] The varied subject-matter and the broad spectrum of social types generally portrayed are accompanied by a wide range of styles and metrical forms to suit

[19] According to Lope himself, 'la cólera/ de un español sentado no se templa' unless he can be shown in two hours everything from the Creation to the Last Judgement. See his verse treatise *Arte nuevo de hacer comedias en este tiempo* (1609), ll.205-08 (*1*, p.131).

[20] 'Los casos de la honra son mejores,/ porque mueven con fuerza a toda gente' (*Arte nuevo*, ll.327-28; *1*, p.134).

[21] The general view was that an *hidalgo* might be a villain but less commonly a figure of fun. Lope defends the introduction of light relief by maintaining that the variety resulting from mingling 'lo cómico' and 'lo trágico' is very pleasing: 'buen ejemplo nos da naturaleza,/ que por tal variedad tiene belleza' (*Arte nuevo*, ll.179-80; *1*, p.130).

the speaker and the occasion.[22] Further variety comes from the introduction of music, songs and sometimes dances: the villagers' welcome for Fernán Gómez, the wedding scene and the celebrations at the Comendador's death provide good pretexts for the songs in *Fuenteovejuna*. Action on the stage is another common feature of the *comedia*, and Lope's use of it in *Fuenteovejuna* is particularly skilful. In Act I there are two incidents involving action on stage, the action in each case being comparatively restrained: firstly Flores and Ortuño attempt to make Pascuala and Laurencia enter the Comendador's house (ll.610-26); the *criados* do not seem to try very hard, and the girls have little difficulty in pushing past them and making their escape. Later, at the end of the act, the Comendador himself seizes Laurencia but is forced to let her go when Frondoso threatens him with his own crossbow (ll.814-32). A violent outcome seems very likely here, but Lope cleverly frustrates the expectations of his audience since Frondoso refuses to be provoked into a fight by the Comendador's furious insults (ll.833-59). These two incidents have their parallels in Act II: firstly when the Comendador's men overcome Mengo, and Fernán Gómez catches Jacinta whom the shepherd had tried to defend (ll.1205-76), and then at the end of the act when Fernán Gómez interrupts the wedding of Laurencia and Frondoso, abducts the bride and arrests the groom (ll.1570-1651). These four widely-spaced examples of on-stage action in Acts I and II show a progressive intensification of violence which reaches a climax in Act III with the angry crowd scenes and the fighting as the mob breaks into the Comendador's house.[23]

The plots of *comedias* were frequently complex, involving deception and disguise, often with women characters dressing up as men, a device popular with the audiences. The tradition of the *mujer varonil* is seen in the warlike activity of the women in Act III of *Fuenteovejuna*, although they do not actually disguise

---

[22] See *Arte nuevo*, ll.246-318 (*1*, pp.132-34).

[23] This intensification of violence is reflected also by the way in which the songs of welcome and the wedding songs associated with the crowd-scenes in Acts I and II have by Act III given way to the screams of an infuriated mob. See *36*, p.30.

themselves.[24] Lope's interweaving of the two actions in this play produces a varied tale of treason, war, tyranny, romance, kidnapping, attempted rape, vengeance, murder and torture, with justice and love finally victorious. Although the story was well known, the dénouement nevertheless holds a surprise, as the idea of the villagers coming to justify themselves before the king and queen is an original notion of Lope's, not found in any other version of the affair.[25] All this, together with occasional excursions into politics or moral philosophy, moments of humour and lyrical passages in praise of simple, rural life, makes up a play which appeals on many levels and must have had something to offer to every member of the very varied public of Lope's time.

[24] Lope claims that 'suele/ el disfraz varonil agradar mucho', but stresses that it is important for such conduct in a woman character to be justified by the situation (*Arte nuevo*, ll.280-83; *1*, p.133). See Melveena McKendrick, *Woman and Society in the Spanish Drama of the Golden Age: a study of the 'mujer varonil'* (Cambridge: Cambridge University Press, 1974).

[25] Lope remarks that if an audience could guess how a play was going to end they would promptly leave the theatre. A sudden and surprising conclusion is common in Golden Age plays. See *Arte nuevo*, ll.234-39; *1*, pp.132-33.

3 *Plot and Sub-plot: their unity and structure*

The fact that *Fuenteovejuna* has a strong main plot and a clearly-defined sub-plot has led some scholars to consider it to be loosely constructed and lacking in unity. Aníbal, for instance, saw the sub-plot as essentially incongruous, involving aristocratic characters as opposed to the more democratic main plot. The sub-plot, he suggested, was an irrelevance for which the only reason was Lope's wish to please his patron the Duque de Osuna who was a member of the Girón family; hence the shifting of the blame for the rebellion from the Maestre to Fernán Gómez and the references to the Maestre's distinguished service later in campaigns against the Moors (ll.515-20 and 2326-37; see *6*, pp.657, 664, 690-91). Sloman, though conceding that the sub-plot was 'linked to the main action in spirit', maintained that it was 'by no means essential to the play' and that 'with but minor alterations, the play could stand with the secondary action removed'.[26] Parker, on the other hand, has shown that although Lope's earlier plays were frequently diffuse and rambling affairs quite lacking in dramatic unity, he eventually began to write in a way which preserved the 'established tradition of multiplicity and variety of incident' (*28*, p.150) yet achieved unity by giving both the main plot and the sub-plot similar themes. *Fuenteovejuna* is an example of such thematic unity: the two plots have a common theme in the rebellion of Fernán Gómez against the established social order, his ill-treatment of the villagers being a microcosm of his villainy against the state: 'Treason and rape are dramatically unified in *Fuenteovejuna* because they are morally akin — aspects of an individual will to social disorder' (*28*, p.146). This point has been taken up in later studies of the play by Ribbans (*31*) and Marín; for Marín the two plots offer an example of hubris on

[26] Albert E. Sloman, 'The Structure of Calderón's *La vida es sueño*', *Modern Language Review*, 48 (1953), 293-300, at p.300.

different levels through 'la violación del orden natural por un individuo a quien las pasiones ciegan y arruinan', and complement each other admirably: 'Lejos de ser superflua, la rebelión política nos da otro punto de vista desde el que contemplar el drama humano, que sin ella perdería una de sus dimensiones' (*23*, pp.63-64).

Fuenteovejuna clearly possesses thematic unity, but scholars who recognise this fact nevertheless tend to deny that the play has much if anything in the way of formal unity as well. Parker maintains that although the Comendador has a prominent role in the two plots they 'remain dramatically independent until they fuse at the end of Act II, when the villagers realize that their only hope of moral freedom lies in the victory of Ferdinand and Isabella in the Civil War. Thereupon, in Act III, they make their vengeance for honour's sake part of the political struggle' (*28*, p.145); Ribbans sees the play as united in theme but 'loose in construction' (*31*, p.163), while for Marín it is 'un caso modelo de intriga secundaria política enlazada *temática pero no orgánicamente* a la principal' (*23*, p.58; my italics). My own view is that *Fuenteovejuna* is in fact a well-shaped play, and that Lope, while linking his plots thematically, further unifies his material by drawing important formal or structural parallels between them.

In the opening scene of Act I (ll.1-172)[27] Lope at once arouses the interest of his audience with the Comendador's mysterious visit to the Maestre: clearly something is afoot, but Lope withholds an explanation while building up an atmosphere of expectancy and tension as Fernán Gómez displays growing impatience at being kept waiting while his sycophantic *criados* endeavour to calm him. The reason for the visit finally emerges in the long speech (ll.69-140) in which Fernán Gómez induces the Maestre to join forces with those opposed to Isabel's succession to the throne and to attack Ciudad Real. Lope's original handling of his subject is now clearly established, and his introduction of a sub-plot dealing with the civil war must have surprised and intrigued those members of the audience (no

---

[27] I follow Casalduero and Ribbans in seeing scene-divisions as indicated by a change in place and time; see *8*, pp.40-42 and *31*, p.150.

doubt the majority) who had supposed that a play entitled *Fuenteovejuna* would simply be about the relationship between Fernán Gómez and the villagers. The Comendador's mention of Fuenteovejuna (l.162) at last brings in the main plot, and his rather condescending description of the inhabitants as 'gente humilde...no enseñada en escuadrones' (ll.163-64) is an effective piece of dramatic irony which would have pleased a public who knew of the fate that was in store for him.

The second scene (ll.173-634) takes place in Fuenteovejuna. Again we start *in medias res*: Laurencia and Pascuala enter, discussing a man, at present away from the village, who has been trying — so far without success — to make Laurencia his mistress. We soon learn that this is the Comendador, that he has seduced other girls (ll.193-95), and that he has been pursuing Laurencia for a month. Mengo, Barrildo and Frondoso now come on stage, deep in argument (l.275), but we remain for a while ignorant of the cause of their disagreement, which turns out to be the nature of love (l.366). There follows a general discussion on love in which Frondoso takes no part, for Lope does not yet wish the audience to know that Frondoso is in love with Laurencia but has been rejected by her, her experiences with the Comendador having made her suspicious of men.[28] Flores now enters to deliver his account of the taking of Ciudad Real; he ignores Laurencia's anxious question as to his master's whereabouts (l.450), and she and the audience must remain in suspense until Flores concludes his speech by announcing the Comendador's return to the village (ll.525-28). Despite the cheerful and ingenuous song greeting the Comendador[29] and the hearty words of welcome spoken by Esteban, the next part of the scene is full of tension arising from the likelihood that Fernán Gómez will very soon attempt once more to seduce Laurencia now that he has returned in a proud and confident mood after his victory. Having impatiently put an abrupt end to the

[28] However, brief hints as to his feelings for Laurencia can be glimpsed in his remarks at ll.436 and 444.

[29] Flores had failed to mention that the capture of Ciudad Real was part of a campaign against the Reyes Católicos, presenting it as a victory over rebels hostile to the Maestre. The villagers seem to suppose that the Comendador has won a victory over the Moors. See ll.537-38.

impromptu ceremony (ll.579-80 and 588-89), he does in fact endeavour to entice Laurencia and Pascuala into his house, but fails as the girls prudently evade his *criados*.

In the first two scenes of Act I Lope presents us successively with two schemes of the Comendador which are already under way when the play opens: one is aimed at dethroning Isabel, the other at dishonouring Laurencia. In the last two scenes (ll.635-722 and 723-859) we see the reaction which his misconduct provokes. Scene three opens with Fernando and Isabel discussing the danger to their realm posed by Afonso of Portugal and his forces; fortunately the Reyes Católicos are able to count on the loyalty of Christian Spain united behind them; as Fernando remarks:

> De Navarra y de Aragón
> está el socorro seguro,
> y de Castilla procuro
> hacer la reformación
> de modo que el buen suceso
> con la prevención se vea. (ll.643-48)

The revolt instigated by Fernán Gómez is now brought to their attention by two *regidores* who have escaped from the massacre in Ciudad Real, and Fernando takes immediate steps to deal with the Comendador's treachery by sending an army to retake the town. The sequence of events in this scene is reflected in the very similar happenings in scene four: this starts with a conversation between Laurencia and Frondoso, a couple who clearly stand out among the villagers. Laurencia is a very beautiful girl and the daughter of the *alcalde* Esteban, while Frondoso is one of the most prosperous and handsome men in Fuenteovejuna:

> tú eres zagal
> de los que huellan brioso
> y, excediendo a los demás,
> vistes bizarro y costoso. (ll.731-34)

They appear to be a popular couple, and the other villagers are
united in their wish to see them happily married soon; in
Laurencia's words:

> en todo el lugar no hay moza
> o mozo en el prado o soto,
> que no se afirme diciendo
> que ya para en uno somos;
> y esperan todos el día
> que el sacristán Juan Chamorro
> nos eche de la tribuna,
> en dejando los piporros. (ll.735-42)

In the main plot Laurencia and Frondoso have a role in some
ways comparable to that of the Reyes Católicos in the sub-plot,
and the esteem in which the village holds them reflects the
national loyalty shown to Fernando and Isabel. Frondoso
assures Laurencia that he truly loves her and longs to marry her,
and her coolness towards him begins to disappear (ll.772-74);
however, at this point Fernán Gómez enters and tries to seize the
girl, a threat with which Frondoso deals by menacing the
Comendador with his own crossbow and forcing him to set her
free.

In Act I Lope integrates his two plots formally by establishing
a series of obvious parallels between them so that each is a
reflexion of the other. The first two scenes show the
Comendador's involvement with the anti-Isabel faction and his
plan to seduce Laurencia; the third and fourth scenes are
identical in structure and show the beginning of counter-moves
aimed at frustrating the villain as Fernando and Frondoso
loyally support the women they love, Frondoso's defiance of
Fernán Gómez mirroring the despatch by Fernando of an army
to retake Ciudad Real. In addition to these structural
symmetries Lope further unifies the main plot and the sub-plot
through the use in each of similar devices such as starting *in
medias res* and delayed revelation as a means of arousing greater
interest.

Having set out very directly and clearly during Act I the issues

at stake in the play, Lope now proceeds to develop them in Act
II. The situation is now far more involved than in Act I:[30]
Frondoso's confrontation with Fernán Gómez has earned him
Laurencia's gratitude and love but also the enmity of the
Comendador, whose lust for the girl is now allied to a desire to
punish and avenge the humiliation inflicted on him by her lover;
political motives — a desire to retain and assert power — are
thus fused in this scene with the sexual motive of the
Comendador's desire for Laurencia. His anger leads him to
offend more of the villagers, who suffer increasing verbal and
physical abuse from him; at the end of the act he alienates the
entire community by interrupting the wedding of Frondoso and
Laurencia and abducting them both. In Act II Lope
appropriately abandons the simple, schematic structure he had
adopted for Act I in favour of something more complex. Less
space is devoted to the sub-plot, essentially only the report by
Cimbranos of the imminent arrival of the royal army at Ciudad
Real (ll.1105-27) and the brief scene (ll.1449-71) in which the
Comendador and Maestre escape as the city falls. However, the
sub-plot begins to be interwoven with the main plot, so that
developments in the conflict between the Comendador and the
Reyes Católicos have repercussions for the inhabitants of
Fuenteovejuna.

At the end of the first scene (ll.860-1136) in which he has
collectively insulted the village men and broken up their
gathering in the square, the Comendador receives Cimbranos's
message and leaves to assist the Maestre in the defence of
Ciudad Real. In the second scene (ll.1137-1276), set in the
country outside the village, he comes upon Jacinta and Mengo.
The audience are reminded of the final scene of Act I as Fernán
Gómez takes the girl away from him. Mengo fails in his attempt
to safeguard her, but this is nonetheless an important moment
for him, as the need to protect Jacinta makes him put aside his
cynical belief or pose that there is no such thing as true love for
another and that all human actions are ruled by self-interest

---

[30] 'En el acto primero ponga el caso,/ en el segundo enlace los sucesos' (*Arte
nuevo*, ll.298-99; *1*, p.133).

since 'nadie tiene amor/ más que a su propia persona' (ll.401-02). The departure of the Comendador affects Frondoso and Laurencia as well, since Frondoso is now able to come out of hiding and show himself in the village again. In the third scene (ll.1277-1448) he proposes to Laurencia who accepts him, and their marriage is warmly approved by her father Esteban and Juan Rojo, Laurencia's uncle and guardian to Frondoso. The callous lack of feeling which the Comendador displayed in the previous scene is followed by a contrasting mood of cordial affection and respect for others: significantly, when Esteban says that the marriage can take place only if Laurencia agrees, Frondoso remarks:

> Justo es, que no hace bien
> quien los gustos atropella. (ll1403-04)

In the fourth scene (ll.1449-71) the Comendador, defeated at Ciudad Real, informs the Maestre that he is returning to Fuenteovejuna (l.1466), a development which is bound to have consequences for the main plot. In the final scene (ll.1472-1651) the audience are kept in a state of tense expectancy by their suspicion that, unknown to the villagers, Fernán Gómez is likely to arrive at any moment, embittered by the loss of Ciudad Real and eager to vent his spite on Frondoso and Laurencia. In a fine *coup de théâtre* he bursts in and halts their wedding celebrations (l.1570). Ironically, the musicians' song about his sexual passions (which the villagers suppose to have been thwarted by the marriage) has just reached the refrain:

> ¿Para qué te ascondes,
> niña gallarda?
> Que mis linces deseos
> paredes pasan. (ll.1566-69)

Laurencia is taken away, Frondoso arrested, and the two plots now come closely together as Esteban warns the Comendador that such abuses are certain to be punished by the Reyes Católicos once the war is over:

> que Reyes hay en Castilla,
> que nuevas órdenes hacen
> con que desórdenes quitan.
> Y harán mal, cuando descansen
> de las guerras, en sufrir
> en sus villas y lugares
> a hombres tan poderosos
> por traer cruces tan grandes. (ll.1620-27)

The audience of course knows what Esteban does not, that the Comendador will in fact be punished by the villagers themselves; however, they rise up against him in the name of the Reyes Católicos and their action thus complements the victory of the royal army over Fernán Gómez at Ciudad Real and contributes to the triumph of order over disorder throughout the realm.

In Act II Lope continues to shape his material with the same care which he had displayed in Act I. Act I has a simple pattern, presenting first the villain's plots against Isabel and Laurencia and then the respective reactions of Fernando and Frondoso; in Act II we find a more complex arrangement of six episodes or incidents of which the last three parallel the first three in reverse order, as the following summary makes clear:

A   The peaceful gathering of the village men is disturbed by Fernán Gómez who orders them to leave the square and go to their homes   (Scene 1)

B   The civil war: Cimbranos brings news of the imminent attack upon Ciudad Real   (Scene 1)

C   Peasant honour and love: Mengo abandons his selfishness and defends Jacinta against the Comendador   (Scene 2)

Ci Peasant honour and love: Frondoso proposes to Laurencia and is accepted; Esteban and Juan Rojo approve   (Scene 3)

Bi The civil war: Ciudad Real falls to the royal army   (Scene 4)

Ai The wedding of Frondoso and Laurencia is disturbed

by Fernán Gómez who arrests the groom and abducts
the bride   (Scene 5)

In Act III the play moves rapidly to its close; the division of
the act into seven scenes gives a greater impression of speed and
urgency than exists in Acts I and II with only four and five
scenes respectively. Once more analysis reveals Lope's concern
for shape and order: again we have a parallelistic structure, this
time in the form of a series of problems to which answers must
quickly be found. Contrary to the audience's expectations, the
royal victory in battle and the death of the Comendador do not
by any means spell the end of the play; rather they raise new
issues of which some in turn spark off others, with the result that
tension and uncertainty are maintained until the final lines and
anti-climax is avoided.[31]

The first scene of Act III (ll.1652-1847) begins with the men of
the village debating what action to take as a result of the
Comendador's latest piece of villainy; their only legal recourse is
to seek the aid of the crown, but this is impossible, given the
Reyes' overriding preoccupation with the civil war (ll.1680-83).
The discussion is interrupted by the arrival of the frenzied
Laurencia who has managed to escape from the Comendador's
house. Lope increases the audience's interest and suspense by
making her describe her experiences in ambiguous terms which
leave it unclear whether or not she has been raped by Fernán
Gómez (ll.1740-52); her bruises and torn clothes are suggestive
but misleading evidence. Laurencia brings news of a fresh
development which necessitates immediate action: the
Comendador is about to hang Frondoso without trial (ll.1784-
87). This, together with her jibes at their unmasculine passivity,

[31] Lope also uses this technique in *Peribáñez y el Comendador de Ocaña*
(1605-12, probably 1605-08): Pedro, the idealized farmer-hero, kills Fadrique,
the Comendador who had tried first to seduce and then to rape Pedro's wife.
Having solved in this way the problem of his personal dishonour, Pedro creates a
fresh problem for himself since he must now answer to the king for slaying an
hidalgo. The villagers of Fuenteovejuna find themselves in a similar position
once they have killed Fernán Gómez. This device of posing new problems once
the central issue of a play has been settled is also used effectively by Calderón,
notably in *El alcalde de Zalamea* and *La vida es sueño*. See J.B. Hall, 'The
Problem of Pride and the Nature of the Evidence in *La vida es sueño*', *Modern
Language Review*, 67 (1982), 339-47.

is enough to make the men resolve to attack Fernán Gómez, and the second scene (ll.1848-1919) portrays the assault on the Comendador's house and his death at the hands of the mob.

Scene three (ll.1920-2027) is set at the royal court, and opens *in medias res* with Manrique concluding his report on the capture of Ciudad Real. No sooner have the king and queen learnt of the success of the campaign, however, than they are faced with a fresh problem as Flores arrives with news of the fate of Fernán Gómez. Fernando's decision to investigate this affair and punish those responsible may at first sight seem surprising, since Fernán Gómez was after all an enemy of the crown. The king, though, is plainly distinguishing his political rebellion from whatever local grievances the villagers may have had against their lord, grievances which should not be settled by murdering him. The king in any case is as yet ignorant of how Fernán Gómez had treated the villagers, the brief comment on his abuses made by the *regidor* of Ciudad Real (ll.691-94) having passed unnoticed under the pressure of what were then more urgent and more important matters; moreover the account of the Comendador's death given by Flores had emphasised the admittedly horrifying details of his murder and mutilation while being studiously vague as to the villagers' motives for such an atrocity ('que vasallos indignados/ con leve causa se atreven', ll.1966-67; cf. note 29, above). Moved to anger by this craftily biased report, the king orders an immediate investigation and the punishment of the murderers 'para ejemplo de las gentes' (l.2021).

In the fourth scene (ll.2028-2124), after the villagers have celebrated the death of Fernán Gómez and sung the praises of the Reyes Católicos, Esteban warns them that the killing of the Comendador is bound to have repercussions for which they must make ready:

> Los Reyes han de querer
> averiguar este caso,
> y más tan cerca del paso
> y jornada que han de hacer.

Concertaos todos a una
en lo que habéis de decir. (ll.2085-90)

At once the villagers rehearse how, even under torture, they will
give nobody away and tell the judge only that 'Fuenteovejuna lo
hizo'. Immediately afterwards the judge's arrival at the village is
announced.

The very brief fifth scene (ll.2125-60) is another which starts
in medias res, a device which increases the sense of speed and
urgency felt throughout this final act. The Maestre has just
learnt of the Comendador's fate, and in a fit of rage announces
his decision to destroy the entire village. The soldier who has
brought the news makes him see reason: the villagers are asking
to be ruled directly by the crown rather than the Order of
Calatrava, and the Maestre cannot dare to offend the Reyes
Católicos a second time:

Señor, tu enojo reporta,
porque ellos al Rey se han dado;
y no tener enojado
al Rey es lo que te importa. (ll.2137-40)

Once again the main plot and the sub-plot come together, and
faced with this new development the Maestre abandons his plan
for vengeance and decides instead to make his peace with
Fernando and Isabel.

As the sixth scene (ll.2161-2289) begins, Laurencia and
Frondoso appear; as at the opening of Act II, Scene 3,
Laurencia is afraid for his safety: then he was in danger from the
Comendador, now he is at risk on account of his involvement in
the death of Fernán Gómez, and Laurencia's words '¿Cómo
estar aquí te atreves?' (l.2176) echo her earlier cry of '¿Cómo así
a venir te atreves/ sin temer tu daño?' (ll.1277-78). Frondoso's
position is certainly difficult, for of all the villagers he had most
reason to hate the Comendador, and did in fact lead the attack
on his house after Fernán Gómez had set him free on condition
that he try to calm the mob. Now the lovers wait uneasily as they
hear the judge interrogating various villagers off stage. This is

one of the most tense scenes of the play: will one of those questioned mention Frondoso's name, or conceivably that of Laurencia who led the women against Fernán Gómez and his *criados*? In quick succession Esteban, a small boy and Pascuala are tortured without result; finally Mengo is questioned, and as he announces his willingness to confess the tension reaches its height, and is then suddenly relieved as Mengo defiantly shouts that 'Fuente Ovejunica' killed the Comendador (l.2249), and the judge abandons the case in despair.

The final scene (ll.2290-2453) is also fast-moving and, like the sixth, has a parallelistic structure. The Maestre comes before the Reyes Católicos, asks their forgiveness and is pardoned; immediately afterwards the judge enters and presents the king with a dilemma: he has been unable to identify any of the Comendador's killers, and Fernando must therefore choose between a general pardon and a massacre of the whole village:

> Y pues tan mal se acomoda
> el poderlo averiguar,
> o los has de perdonar
> o matar la villa toda. (ll.2378-81)

In an unexpected dénouement which owes nothing to traditional versions of the story, the villagers are now brought before the king and queen in order to give an account of themselves. As with the Maestre, the blame for their action is shown to be the Comendador's: Esteban briefly describes the Comendador's general ill-treatment of the village, and Frondoso and Mengo describe what they had suffered as individuals; it is only now that the audience learns that Laurencia had not after all been dishonoured by Fernán Gómez (ll.2410-13). The surprise of this delayed revelation and the broad humour of Mengo's account of his beating are effective ways of keeping the audience attentive and interested until the very end of the play. The king gives as his motive for granting a pardon what Pring-Mill has called the legal loophole of the judge's failure to obtain a confession or denunciation (*29*, p.30), but we may reasonably infer that his decision is influenced as well by what the villagers have just told him.[32] If Fernando does not actually say as much this is partly because it is obvious, partly because with a traditionally impatient public final speeches had to be brief so as not to delay the conclusion of a *comedia* once the resolution of the plot had become apparent.[33]

Each of the three acts of *Fuenteovejuna* has its own distinctive pattern; Lope has ordered his material with care, giving it symmetry largely through the use of formal parallels to unify each act, to link incidents in different acts, and to integrate the main plot and the sub-plot. The structural unity of the play is further exemplified by two sequences of parallel events not discussed in the foregoing scene-by-scene analysis. The uprising fomented by the Comendador in Acts I and II and the revolt of the village in Act III have an identical pattern, and there is thus both dramatic irony and poetic justice in the overthrow and death of the villain in a rebellion which echoes the rebellion he had himself earlier organised against Fernando and Isabel. In each case we start with the instigation of the revolt, so that Laurencia's impassioned speech to the village men recalls the Comendador's harangue to the Maestre; next the rebels organise their forces and then there is a siege, the attack on the house of Fernán Gómez corresponding to the capture of Ciudad Real, while his ignominious death is an ironic echo of the atrocities inflicted by the Calatravans on the inhabitants of the city. A request for appropriate action is now made to the king and queen by the *regidores* of Ciudad Real in Act I and by Flores in Act III. Fernando and Isabel react by sending an army to retake Ciudad Real and the judge to investigate the death of Fernán Gómez. In the subsequent confrontations the Comendador and Maestre are defeated by the royal army whereas in a reversal of the pattern the people of Fuenteovejuna triumph over the judge. Finally the Maestre and the villagers, victims in their different ways of the villainy of Fernán Gómez, are pardoned by the

---

[32] This was of course the reason for the pardon given in the account of Rades y Andrada. See Chapter 1, above.

[33] Judgements by monarchs at the end of Golden Age plays tend to be brief. Again, Lope's *Peribáñez* and Calderón's *El alcalde de Zalamea* offer good examples; cf. also Segismundo's sentence on the rebel soldier in *La vida es sueño*.

Reyes Católicos.[34]

It is thus possible to see *Fuenteovejuna* as having two successive actions, portraying similar series of events, as well as having (which is the more usual interpretation) 'two parallel actions which develop side by side, the one reflecting the other, so that the Comendador's cruelty towards the villagers is a microcosm of his villainy towards the state' (*12*, p.57). Whichever way we look at the play it is unreasonable to deny its formal artistry or to see it as loosely constructed. The thematic unity of *Fuenteovejuna* is complemented by a structural unity in which the different elements in the story are blended into a balanced and orderly whole. In a triumph of *disposición* or arrangement, Lope has created a work of art which succeeds in reconciling the conflicting ideals of *unidad* and *variedad*. Contemporary theorists recommended this and the better artists endeavoured to put the precept into practice, albeit not always as successfully as Lope did on this occasion.

[34] For a more detailed account of the similarities between the two revolts, see *12*, pp.57-59.

4 *Characterization*

Like other Golden Age dramatists Lope was concerned to offer his public what Parker has called a 'complete action' rather than a 'series of complete characters'.[35] This concept of the primacy of action over character drawing must not be misunderstood: obviously the action of a play like *Fuenteovejuna* is determined by the kind of people the characters are and by the manner in which they choose to behave, since Golden Age drama takes for granted the notions of free will and moral responsibility. Man, for Lope and his contemporaries, is not the plaything of fate or the victim of some inevitable destiny, despite the acknowledged influence of temperament and environment. However, in the comparatively short, fast-moving kind of play which Lope popularized, the detailed analysis and elaboration of character were hardly possible. His deliberate technique was to present characters who, even when they are full of energy and dominate the play as Fernán Gómez does, still remain types.[36] They are not complete in the sense of being full or rounded, but are simple or flat rather than multi-faceted. Apart from falling in love or being provoked from passivity to action they tend not to develop as the play progresses. They can usually be identified readily as villains or heroes, the former having few good qualities and the latter few faults. Once they know what they must do, they set about achieving their aims with singleminded thoroughness. The more mixed or complex characters and the frequently baffling moral dilemmas that appear later in the work of Calderón are less a feature of Lope's plays which usually have a more straightforward view of life. What makes Lope's

[35] *The Approach to the Spanish Drama of the Golden Age* (see note 13, above), p.5.

[36] All that Lope says on characterization in the *Arte nuevo* (ll.269-93; *1*, pp.132-33) is that characters should speak according to type. Thus the speeches of the king must be suitably dignified, those of old men modest and edifying, those of lovers passionate and moving. See *2*, p.xvi.

characters so vivid is the power of their passions and beliefs, which in *Fuenteovejuna* leads to violent conflict as the treachery and lust of Fernán Gómez are confronted by the loyalty and love displayed by the villagers; the problems which the villagers face arise not from any contradiction or inconsistency within themselves as individuals — as often happens in Calderón — but from the actions of a villain upon whose removal harmony and tranquillity are soon restored.

The above does not imply that because Lope's characters are types they are not presented carefully and skilfully. Lope's concept of character tended to rule out complexity and development but he had other ways of keeping the public interested in his characters, and modern readers and audiences should not condemn him for failing to achieve what it was never his intention to do. With this in mind we can now consider the characters in *Fuenteovejuna*.

Fernán Gómez

In all he does the Comendador obeys the dictates of instinct and passion rather than those of conscience and reason. Pride is a central element in his character: the opening lines of the play reveal his obsession with his name and his rank (ll.1-9); no villager can compare with a man like himself (ll.1254-55), and the people of Fuenteovejuna and their affairs are in his eyes merely 'cosas tan viles' (l.1217). A related obsession is his yearning for violence and domination both on a national level and in his personal relationships. Like so many other proud, obsessed and thus unbalanced characters in Golden Age literature, he exteriorises his internal disorders by projecting them upon society.[37] However, his obsessions inevitably impair his perception of reality, and he cannot see that his schemes are bound to fail, for the power of a united Spain and the solidarity and moral strength of the villagers could never be overcome by

[37] Don Quijote is the best-known instance in Golden Age writing of an obsession which leads to an impaired perception of reality; with his compulsive urge to 'negar la sangre', Pablos in Quevedo's *Buscón* is clearly another. Similar examples in the plays of Calderón include Gutierre in *El médico de su honra*, Curcio in *La devoción de la Cruz*, Basilio and the unregenerate Segismundo in *La vida es sueño*. See my article referred to in note 31, above.

one man, however arrogant and daring.

The Comendador's tempestuous nature emerges at once in the opening scene of Act I: his two *criados* are plainly nervous and afraid of his ill-temper while he rages at being kept waiting by the Maestre; as Téllez Girón finally enters to greet him, the Comendador abruptly complains of the discourtesy shown him (ll.44-51), answering the Maestre's respectful apologies merely with the curt and condescending comment 'De vos estoy satisfecho' (l.64). His subsequent speech (ll.69-140), urging the Maestre to join the anti-Isabel faction and attack Ciudad Real, is his longest in the play; it is quite unlike his speeches on other occasions to his *criados* and the villagers, which are brief to the point of insolence and largely take the form of terse questions, exclamations, oaths, insults and peremptory commands. His social inferiors he can browbeat but the Maestre, a fellow-aristocrat and his senior in the Order though lacking in years and experience, has to be persuaded. The Comendador's analysis of the political situation is perfunctory: without examining them he dismisses Isabel's claims in a few words ('no con derecho tan claro/ a vuestros deudos', ll.98-99), appealing instead to the young man's loyalty to his relatives who support the Pretender, and playing upon his sense of insecurity and his lack of experience and achievement which supposedly make him as yet unworthy of the name and rank he bears (ll.117-20, 129-35). Fernán Gómez does not long maintain the pretence of offering advice to a superior ('vengo a aconsejaros', l.104): he takes it for granted that the Maestre will do as he proposes ('Poca gente es menester', l.111; 'Será bien que deis asombro', l.117), and finally issues the direct commands which typify his normal mode of discourse ('Mirad los Condes de Urueña,/ de quien venís', ll.121-22; 'Sacad esa blanca espada', l.129).

When at the end of the act Fernán Gómez attempts to seduce Laurencia he again clearly expects that his wishes will be obeyed; in a short speech (ll.786-804), he does not bother with persuasion but intimidates her from the start. After a passing reference to the girl's beauty he offensively refers to her as a 'monster', since her attractions seem to promise favours which she does not grant; he threateningly adds that she cannot escape him here in the countryside and (as he thinks) far from help; he insists that she shall not slight her lord by refusing him what he desires, and ends by boasting of his conquest of other village women.

There is a marked contrast between this speech and Frondoso's earlier declaration of love and offer of marriage (ll.751-57, 767-71). Love is something which the Comendador cannot understand;[38] instead he seeks merely to gratify his lust in the pursuit of women whom he seduces and then abandons; this is a form of sport which gives him pleasure similar to that of the chase and which reduces women to the status of animals. Appropriately he is out hunting when he finds Laurencia, and his words on seeing her suggest that she is for him no more than another potential victim to be added to his trophies:

> No es malo venir siguiendo
> un corcillo temeroso,
> y topar tan bella gama. (ll.779-81; see also ll.949-64)

Like don Juan in Tirso de Molina's *El burlador de Sevilla* whom in many ways he anticipates, Fernán Gómez takes a sadistic pleasure in the dishonouring and humiliation of women (ll.1081-84 and 1095-1102); once they have served their purpose he rejects them with the same cynical lack of feeling which he displays to his other dupe the Maestre whom he abandons as Ciudad Real falls with the laconic remark '*Tus* desinios, Girón, quedan perdidos' (l.1456; my italics).

A man of deeds rather than words, the Comendador generally prefers to achieve his aims through action, and on being rebuffed by Laurencia he at once assaults her physically ('a la prática de manos/ reduzgo melindres', ll.816-17), just as later in Act II he carries off Jacinta and has Frondoso and Laurencia seized by his followers. When people stand up to him or criticize his conduct in unanswerable terms his usual reaction is one of violence: so he dismisses the village men to their homes when Esteban and the

---

[38] Wardropper (*37*, pp.166-67) points out that Fernán Gómez uses the word 'amor' only twice, and then in the sense of the loyalty which a subordinate owes to his superior (ll.12, 546). There is in fact a third example, when he describes himself (l.1095) as 'de amores loco', but this is simply a reference to his lust.

regidor condemn his immorality towards the womenfolk (ll.1009-20), has Mengo flogged for defending Jacinta (ll.1244-50), and beats Esteban with his own rod of office when the *alcalde* warns him that the Reyes Católicos will not tolerate his abuses (ll.1631-34). When he does endeavour to justify his actions, his arguments are so slight as to be unworthy of serious consideration (ll.1594-1606 and 1617-18).[39] The Comendador seems on the whole an unintelligent and unperceptive man: as the play opens he typically fails to notice how Ortuño and Flores comically contradict each other over the Maestre's apparent lack of courtesy ('Está, con la edad, más grave', l.3; 'Es muchacho, no te asombre', l.6), and then does not see that Flores's remark about Téllez Girón is also a sly comment on how he himself treats his subordinates:

> Llaman la descortesía
> necedad en los iguales,
> porque es entre desiguales
> linaje de tiranía. (ll.25-28; see *29*, p.11)

In Act II, he seems genuinely amazed that Frondoso should have dared to menace him with a crossbow to protect Laurencia (ll.1044-49). Incapable of realising that even commoners have their own sense of honour (ll.987-88), he has to ask Mengo what the people of Fuenteovejuna think about him (ll.1237-38), and shows what appears to be unfeigned surprise when the village finally turns against him in Act III ('¿El pueblo, contra mí?', l.1860).

Another aspect of the Comendador's character is his perversity: Mengo refers to him as a 'perverso Nerón' (l.2422), and examples of his warped sense of values abound throughout the play. We have already seen how he debases love to a mere brutal sport, a source of cruel amusement; in addition he corrupts the young Maestre and perverts the ideals of the Order of Calatrava by using its forces to make war not on the infidel but on Spain's Christian

---

[39] It is possible that he is not advancing them seriously himself, in which case he is insulting the intelligence of the villagers. For the narrowly legalistic nature of his attempt at self-justification, see below, Chapter 6.

rulers; as Flores remarks in his account of the capture of Ciudad
Real:

> ....la Cruz roja obliga
> cuantos al pecho la tienen,
> aunque sean de orden sacro,
> mas contra moros se entiende. (ll.465-68)

This misuse of the Order in the sub-plot is reflected in the main
plot by a number of incidents in which Fernán Gómez puts
material objects to ends other than those for which they were
intended: Mengo, for example, is bound with his own sling before
being flogged, so that his means of defence is turned against him
(ll.1233-35); Mengo later describes this to the villagers and
mentions another atrocity, which turned a medical treatment into
a form of torture:

> Pero que le hayan echado
> una melecina a un hombre,
> que, aunque no diré su nombre,
> todos saben que es honrado,
> llena de tinta y chinas.
> ¿Cómo se puede sufrir? (ll.1491-96)

Later, at the close of Act II, the Comendador makes the wedding
into an occasion for sorrow instead of rejoicing ('¡Volvióse en
luto la boda!', ll.1642), and strips the *alcalde* Esteban of his staff
of office with which he then beats him, so that the symbol of
honour and authority becomes a source of humiliation (ll.1631-
34). Ironically, Fernán Gómez meets his death at the hands of
people, who, thanks to him, have in a sense become perverted: the
ordinarily peaceful village folk whom he had once described as
'no enseñada en escuadrones' (l.164) attack him and his followers
with merciless rage, and even the women form a band of
'amazonas'.

As St Thomas Aquinas points out, all created things are
directed by God towards ends which are appropriate to their
form, so that to pervert such ends is to violate the divinely-

appointed natural order and thus to do injury to God himself.[40]
The Comendador, then, is a rebel against God as well as against
human society. His speech to the Maestre describes the young
man's ancestors as dwelling not in the traditional Christian
Heaven but in a kind of Valhalla, and there is a suggestive pagan
ring to such expressions as 'mostrando/ os están desde la fama/
los laureles que ganaron' (ll.122-24), 'las alas de la fama' (l.127)
and 'templo inmortal/ de vuestros claros pasados' (ll.139-40). The
mention of the cross which is the emblem of the Order of
Calatrava ignores its Christian symbolism and stresses instead its
red colour, which allegedly justifies war and bloodshed (ll.129-
37). As the play progresses and examples of the Comendador's
immorality and sadism multiply, he is presented more and more
frequently as an enemy of religion, likened to the Devil (ll.810-13,
1143-44), to pagan tyrants such as Heliogabalus and Nero
(ll.1173-76, 2422), and called a barbarian (ll.1485, 1668, 1701) and
'malo cristiano' (l.1883), while warnings of divine punishment
and references to divine intervention proliferate (ll.1007-08,
1146-47, 1251-52, 1275-76, 1577, 1641, 1657, 1702-03).[41] The
defeat and death of the Comendador must have reminded Golden
Age audiences of the ultimate superiority of the powers of good
over those of evil; as Moir puts it: 'In what is basically a religious
drama, we delight in his destruction and we experience a type of
Christian triumph' (*27*, p.542). Only in his dying appeal to God's
mercy (l.1895) does the Comendador come to recognize his follies
and possibly to repent of them.

Another aspect of the villainy of Fernán Gómez is his
treachery: a traitor to the Reyes Católicos, he also betrays the
trust of the women whom he seduces (ll.193-95), and the loyalty
which the villagers are still prepared to show him when he returns
from the capture of Ciudad Real (ll.529-94). Furthermore he is
untrue to the vows of poverty, chastity and obedience which he
would have taken on entering the Order of Calatrava (*27*, p.542).

---

[40] See for example *Summa theologica*, I (i), qu.22, art.2, and (ii), qu.94, art.3; also
II (ii), qu.154, art.12. For the Comendador's perversity see also *12*, pp.65-66.

[41] The manuscript *Historia de Córdoba* of Andrés Morales (1620) alleges that the
Reyes saw the Comendador's death as 'castigo del cielo'. See *21*, p.534.

Interestingly, the term 'traidor' is not used of him before the
village uprising in Act III, when it occurs no fewer than seven
times in under two hundred lines (ll.1727, 1777, 1813, 1814, 1866,
1883, 1894). By emphasizing the Comendador's treachery at this
point in the play, Lope was no doubt endeavouring to make the
revolt against him more justified in the eyes of a public for whom
treason was particularly abhorrent — to such an extent, Lope tells
us in the *Arte nuevo*, that actors who played traitors' parts ran the
risk of being refused service by merchants and of being generally
ostracized (*Arte nuevo*, ll.331-34; *1*, p.134).

Lope justifies the villagers' uprising still further by presenting
Fernán Gómez as a tyrant; just as he stressed his treachery so
Lope emphasizes the tyranny of the Comendador in the third act:
in Acts I and II 'tirano' is not used at all, and 'tiranía' appears
once only (l.28), whereas in Act III both words are brought in
time and again (ll.1697, 1711, 1726, 1776, 1808, 1813, 1814, 1877,
1878, 1968, 2030, 2042, 2053, 2056, 2067, 2080, 2394). This would
suggest that Lope agreed with those contemporary authorities
who maintained that rebellion was permissible against a tyrant.[42]
Inspired possibly by Rades y Andrada's reference to 'las tyranías
del Comendador Mayor, por las quales avía merescido la muerte'
(see above, Chapter 1), Lope gives Fernán Gómez the traditional
characteristics of the tyrant as defined by Aquinas in his *De
regimine principum*.[43] Thus the Comendador is indifferent to the
good of others and is concerned only with his own selfish ends,
oppressing people according to his ruling passions: Aquinas
instances greed and anger, and Lope gives numerous examples of
the latter, adding to them the sexual lust suggested by Rades y
Andrada. For Aquinas, tyrants seek to damage the moral
character of their subjects, since they fear that virtue in others is a
threat to their own unjust rule; this point seems to be echoed in

[42] Although some scholars (including Quevedo) felt that tyrants should not be
resisted by force, others disagreed. For Gómez-Mariana, 'parece afirmar Lope el
derecho a la oposición, si bien encauzada siempre dentro de las normas dictadas
por la filosofía tradicional — por Aristóteles y Tomás de Aquino sobre todo —,
normas que eran recordadas en su tiempo de nuevo por el P. Vitoria y Domingo de
Soto en la Universidad de Salamanca' (*11*, p.57).

[43] See *De regimine principum*, I, chs 3, 6-7, ed. Dino Bigongiari in *The Political
Ideas of St Thomas Aquinas*, The Hafner Library of Classics, 15 (New York:
Hafner, 1953), pp.183-90.

Laurencia's speech on how 'lenguas descorteses' (she has the Comendador in mind), treat with mockery and contempt those who, like her, wish to lead moral lives (ll.328-48). Aquinas further maintains that tyrants follow a policy of divide and rule, endeavouring to sow discord among their people and to spoil friendly relationships so that mutual trust is destroyed and no plot against the tyrant can be formed; in this way, he says, tyrants try to prevent marriages and feasting. The conduct of Fernán Gómez conforms to this pattern, for he harms various marriages by his lust, attempts to prevent the marriage of Frondoso and Laurencia, and disrupts the wedding feast just as he had earlier put an end to the gathering of the men in the square.[44]

The Comendador, to conclude, is an impressive study in villainy; his villainy manifests itself in different ways, with the consequence that although he remains a type the exploration of his personality offers something of the variety found in a more complex, many-sided character. Similarly, the progressive revelation of the range and depth of his wickedness approximates to the interest which derives from the contemplation of a character who genuinely undergoes development and change.

The Maestre

Rodrigo Téllez Girón is a youth of eighteen, and as such conforms to the contemporary literary stereotype which requires a young man to be headstrong and passionate. This tendency is especially marked in young *hidalgos*, since it was believed to be harder in the artificial environment of the town and court for men to lead a moral existence than in the country; the peasant lived a simpler life, relatively free from temptation, and ruled by an ordered pattern of daily work and acts of devotion (see for example Laurencia's description of her day: ll.215-48).

The Maestre has his good qualities: he is certainly brave, and displays as well the formal courtesy expected in an *hidalgo* and so noticeably lacking in Fernán Gómez (ll.41-44, 59-63). However, his youthful craving for excitement and his eagerness to acquire fame and honour, the traditional prerogatives of the nobleman,

[44] For a fuller account of the question of tyranny in *Fuenteovejuna*, see *12*, pp.60-65.

make him accept unquestioningly the Comendador's proposals: in his brutal treatment of the citizens of Ciudad Real (ll.506-12) he is uncritically following the advice of Fernán Gómez that he should show no mercy to his foes, in order to obtain the reputation of a man to be feared, despite his youth (ll.117-20). When the royal army defeats the Calatravans at Ciudad Real in Act II, he is unable or unwilling to see this as poetic justice, and naively blames instead the workings of blind fate: '¿Qué puedo hacer, si la fortuna ciega/ a quien hoy levantó, mañana humilla?' (ll.1457-58; see *29*, p.15).

The Maestre's immaturity is apparent also in his fit of rage on learning of the Comendador's death; he is first tempted to kill the innocent messenger and then announces his intention to take an army and raze Fuenteovejuna to the ground (ll.2131-36). Only on learning that the villagers have asked to be placed under the direct rule of the crown does he begin to see some political sense and to realize that he cannot afford to displease the Reyes Católicos a second time. This leads to a recognition of his moral errors, and he prudently decides to seek the forgiveness of the king and queen and thus to regain the honour which he has forfeited through his rebellion (ll.2157-60). Before Fernando and Isabel the Maestre is both humble and dignified. He comes at once to the point and asks for pardon; mentioning that he was led astray by Fernán Gómez, he yet acknowledges his own responsibility, and promises henceforth to put his courage and the forces of his Order to better use in the wars against the Moors of Granada. The audience's final impression of him is that of a potentially worthy man who has seen the error of his ways and is determined to make amends, and there seems no reason to query Manrique's sympathetic comment that 'aunque es en edad pequeño,/ es valeroso soldado' (ll.2308-09).

Flores and Ortuño

The Comendador's *criados* are an unprincipled and unpleasant pair of bullies whose primary function seems to be that of pimping for their master and facilitating his affairs with the village women. Their relationship with Fernán Gómez is

sufficiently intimate for him to criticize the Maestre in their
presence, but they nonetheless fear him, as their nervousness at
the start of Act I suggests, and as is indicated more plainly later by
Flores's words when they fail to lure Laurencia and Pascuala into
the Comendador's house:

> ¡Muy buen recado llevamos!
> No se ha de poder sufrir
> lo que nos ha de decir
> cuando sin ellas nos vamos. (ll.627-30)

Both are sycophantic, especially Flores who is very quick to
humour his master, boasting of his attack on a man he thought
was Frondoso (ll.1031-36), insulting the villagers (ll.1219-22) and
hypocritically referring to the Comendador's plan to hang
Frondoso without trial as an act of justice (ll.1854-55). Neither of
them, however, is above criticizing Fernán Gómez, albeit in a
sufficiently oblique way for him to fail to grasp the point (ll.17-
22, 23-28).

Flores seems the more important of the two, and perhaps the
more intelligent, discussing the nature of sexual attraction and
quoting Aristotle (ll.1085-94), and craftily giving the villagers and
the Reyes Católicos detailed yet misleading accounts of the
capture of Ciudad Real (ll.455-524) and the killing of the
Comendador (ll.1948-2013). His assertion that the latter incident
was 'la mayor crueldad/ que se ha visto entre las gentes' (ll.1952-
53), is a particularly hypocritical piece of exaggeration when we
set the action of the villagers against the slaughter carried out by
the Comendador and Maestre in Ciudad Real.

Despite the occasional coarsely comic line (see for example
ll.615-25), they are not amusing characters but rather a couple of
immoral toughs who will not scruple to do anything to please their
master and thus profit themselves. Pring-Mill's view of them as
picaresque types serving a villain for what they can get out of it
(*29*, p.12) sums them up very well.

The people of Fuenteovejuna

In contrast with the evil and disruptive Comendador, they are identified with order, harmony and good. Although when provoked they will fight to defend their loved ones, they are ruled more by reason and prudence than by instinct. Time and again they are shown discussing issues together (as in the debate on love and the meeting of the *junta*), listening to other points of view, offering and accepting advice. Significantly, no fewer than forty-two out of sixty-three *sentencias* (i.e. general moralizing remarks) in the play are made by them (*29*, pp.6, 9). This elevated moral view of the villagers reflects the contemporary literary notion of the superiority of *aldea* over *corte*; other examples of this idealization include certain proper names such as Frondoso, Laurencia and Leonelo, stylistic *cultismos*, and of course the philosophical debate on love in Act I, reminiscent of such discussions in pastoral literature. However, the idealization is not taken too far: proper names such as Mengo, Esteban and Pascuala, and examples of rustic and at times archaic vocabulary and turns of phrase ensure that the villagers remain recognizable members of a Spanish rural community; Fuenteovejuna is perhaps a more prosperous village than most, but it has its 'simples labradores' (l.1705) as well as its richer 'gente muy principal' (l.980), it possesses its properly-elected local officials, and life there follows a typical pattern of farming and domestic tasks, with shepherds like Mengo tending their flocks, other men concerned with the crops (ll.860-91), and the women washing garments at the stream and preparing meals (ll.215-48, 723-26; see *21*, pp.519-23).

As the play develops, the village itself gradually assumes the identity of a character, becoming what López Estrada calls 'el personaje colectivo que es representación de una comunidad o pueblo' (*21*, p.536). While the misconduct of Fernán Gómez becomes more frequent and more serious, so a growing sense of love and solidarity brings the villagers together: Frondoso's defence of Laurencia leads to her recognizing the extent of his feelings for her and accepting his proposal of marriage, while Mengo puts aside his air of cynical egoism and defends Jacinta;

the number of crowd-scenes increases, with the marriage-feast, the meeting of the village council, the attack by the mob on the Comendador's house, and the scenes of mass rejoicing afterwards. The villagers' new-found sense of corporate loyalty is a practical manifestation of the theoretical belief in unselfish love for others advanced in the debate in Act I, and it survives the test of the tortures inflicted by the judge on men and women, young and old. Their solidarity is a microcosm of the unity of all Christian Spain under the Reyes Católicos in whose name they rose against Fernán Gómez. As Kirschner points out, this national unity is strongly emphasized in the final scene of Act III: 'La comedia termina con la masa y los Reyes Católicos acompañados de su séquito en la escena y con la integración a la Corona de todas las fuerzas operantes' (*15*, p.143).

The importance of the idea of the collective protagonist should not be exaggerated, however: Esteban's general account of the various ways in which Fernán Gómez had offended the community (ll.2391-2401) is followed by Frondoso's description to the Reyes of how he and Laurencia suffered at the Comendador's hands, after which Mengo tells of the flogging he received for Jacinta's sake. The audience is thus reminded of the outrages endured by specific members of the village, who have their own particular grievances resulting from personal shame and dishonour. The play is as much about the restoration of individual honour as the acquisition and triumphant assertion of a collective consciousness among the villagers as a body, no doubt for the simple reason that an audience would find it easier to identify with one or two characters — especially a pair of endangered lovers — than with an undifferentiated mass.

Laurencia and Frondoso

The heroine and hero of the play, they stand somewhat apart from the other villagers by reason of their rather literary names and their superior status in the community. Their role in the main plot is comparable to that of the Reyes in the sub-plot, and it is they who in the final scene comment on the splendour and majesty of Fernando and Isabel (ll.2386-89); Frondoso speaks the closing lines of the play, acknowledging in the name of the village the pardon granted them by the king. Like the Reyes, Laurencia and Frondoso are praised in *coplas* sung by the villagers, wishing them a long life. The main plot is in essence the story of the conflict between the two lovers and Fernán Gómez who has been attempting to seduce Laurencia even before the play begins; they are highly popular in the village, and when the Comendador breaks up their wedding he offends all the inhabitants who had for so long been hoping that they would marry. Though they are angered by the Comendador's other misdeeds, it is essentially to save Frondoso's life that the villagers rebel, spurred on by the anguished Laurencia who at that stage appears to have been raped by the villain. In the torture scene the great fear of Laurencia and Frondoso is doubtless that somebody will give way and denounce one or both of them as responsible for the death of the Comendador. As is made plain by their last exchange at the end of this scene (ll.2282-89), the steadfastness of their fellow-villagers removes the threat to their continued happiness which was hanging over them when the scene began.

Laurencia is perhaps more important than Frondoso; indeed, she has the most extensive part in the play, slightly longer even than that of the Comendador. Like so many heroines in Golden Age drama, she is a forceful personality, something of a *mujer varonil*: her maturity and moral strength which enable her to resist the Comendador's advances contrast strongly with the weakness of the Maestre who has been easily suborned. However, her experiences with Fernán Gómez turn her sensible preference for a simple, honest life (ll.215-48) into an extreme distrust of all men ('¡No fiarse de ninguno!', l.273). Thus the malign influence of the Comendador upsets normal human relationships in the village, for Laurencia seems incapable of recognizing true love, and is consumed with bitterness and suspicion as her speech denouncing 'lenguas descorteses' suggests (ll.328-48). Particularly poignant is the incident during the debate on love in which Mengo, seeking to prove that all love is self-interest, puts a series of questions to Laurencia and, innocently twisting the knife in the wound, thereby reminds her of how Fernán Gómez desires her only for his own pleasure:

MENGO: ¿Qué es amor?
LAURENCIA: Es un deseo
              de hermosura.
MENGO: Esa hermosura
              ¿por qué el amor la procura?
LAURENCIA: Para gozarla.
MENGO: Eso creo.
              Pues ese gusto que intenta,
              ¿no es para él mismo?
LAURENCIA: Es así.
MENGO: Luego, ¿por quererse a sí
              busca el bien que le contenta?
LAURENCIA: Es verdad.
MENGO: Pues de ese modo
              no hay amor, sino el que digo,
              que por mi gusto le sigo,
              y quiero dármelo en todo. (ll.409-20)

Determined that she will love nothing save her own honour
(l.435), Laurencia spurns Frondoso and disappoints both his
hopes and the expectations of the villagers (ll.723-50). When he
offers marriage and defies the Comendador for her sake she
begins to have a kinder opinion of him (ll.1154-59); she is quick to
accept his second proposal ('Pues a la villa y a ti/ respondo que lo
seremos', ll.1303-04), and at once becomes more lighthearted and
carefree than before, playfully hiding with Frondoso as her father
and Juan Rojo approach, and then laughing at Esteban's little
joke at her expense (ll.1421-22).

This happiness is shortlived; early in Act III there is a reversal
of the situation at the end of Act I as Laurencia is forced to save
Frondoso from the Comendador. The strength of her character
and that wit or intelligence which Mengo had noticed in her
(ll.351-52) are apparent in her address to the *junta*: vehement and
excited though this is, it is not the speech of someone who has lost
all control, but rather a shrewd appeal deftly calculated to have
the desired effect upon its hearers. Turning first to Esteban,
Laurencia reminds him of his obligation to avenge the wrongs she
has suffered, since her marriage is unconsummated and she

therefore still remains in his care (ll.1721-39); she then directs her scorn at the others present who witnessed her abduction and yet did nothing to prevent it; after condemning their lack of common humanity (ll.1753-67), national pride (ll.1768-69) and masculinity (ll.1770-83), she suddenly informs them that Frondoso is about to be hanged without trial and that Fernán Gómez intends afterwards to massacre them all (ll.1784-88); before they can recover from this shock she follows it with a fierce attack on their unmanly passivity, a form of cowardice which she and the village women at least will never display (ll.1789-93).

With the village women themselves, Laurencia finds that she has less need of her powers of persuasion; her vigorous personality and her authority emerge here in the way in which she allots quasi-military ranks to Jacinta and Pascuala, and firmly turns down two unnecessary proposals which Pascuala puts forward (ll.1816-47). She keeps her troops well under control in the fight at the Comendador's house, posting them to guard the entrance and deal with any of the enemy who try to escape, while she goes in alone to join the men of the village. After the Comendador's death Laurencia must still endure uncertainty and fear for Frondoso's safety and perhaps her own. Only when the judge's investigation fails can she enjoy once more with her husband the laughter and happiness which she had experienced briefly in Act II (ll.2282-89).

Frondoso is first linked with Laurencia not romantically but morally when each of them comments on the contemporary tendency to turn moral values upside down, a failing which for Laurencia is characteristic of *corte* rather than *aldea* (ll.321-23); he gives examples of how hypocrites praise in others qualities which they really know to be defects, and she condemns those for whom every virtue in others is a vice (ll.292-320, 328-48). Thus Lope presents them as a pair of kindred spirits sharing a common concern for honesty and sincerity. These qualities distinguish Frondoso's love for Laurencia (Esteban congratulates him on 'la limpieza de tu celo', l.1380), which is completely free from self-interest or thoughts of material advantage — he twice refuses, for instance, to receive a dowry from her father (ll.1397-98, 1435-36). Unlike Fernán Gómez, Frondoso is always in control of his passions: guided by love rather than lust, he wants an honourable and permanent relationship with Laurencia in marriage; in his encounter with the Comendador Frondoso is certainly both angry and offended (l.827) but he restrains his feelings, and his bearing is calm and correct: he refuses to be provoked by insults (l.830), stresses that his defiance of the Comendador is only the natural result of his love for Laurencia (ll.843-45), and prudently declines the challenge which Fernán Gómez issues. As a commoner he cannot fight a duel with his social superior, and his words 'Yo me conformo/ con mi estado' (ll.851-52) are an oblique reminder of how Fernán Gómez by contrast fails to live up to the obligations which his own status imposes on him.

In the final act Frondoso's *copla* in praise of the Reyes Católicos (ll.2035-42) and his foretelling of better times under their rule (ll.2076-77) are a further reminder of the links between himself and Laurencia on the one hand and Fernando and Isabel on the other. His loyalty to the Crown matches his loyalty towards Laurencia and the other villagers, which causes him to return to Fuenteovejuna despite his personal danger while the judge is carrying out enquiries:

> ¿Es bien que los demás deje
> en el peligro presente,
> y de tu vista me ausente? (ll.2191-93)

This sense of loyalty (l.1295) is perhaps Frondoso's outstanding characteristic and is unwittingly acknowledged by Fernán Gómez when, intending an insult, he calls Frondoso a dog, the most loyal animal of all (l.830).

Other villagers

Esteban would offer a good part for the *barba*, the actor who specialised in old men's roles. As a loving father he has some touching speeches: Frondoso's request for the hand of Laurencia gives him great joy, and also a sense of relief that here is a lover who, unlike the Comendador, wishes only to honour his daughter (ll.1373-86); at the meeting of the *junta* he expresses both his personal grief at dishonour and also shame as a patriot that such things could take place in his 'patria sin honra, ya perdida' (l.1665). He is a man distinguished by virtue both in his private life and in his public capacity as *alcalde*, defending the rights of the villagers, reminding them of their duties and acting as their spokesman before both the Comendador and the Reyes. So far as the action goes, his main contribution is to prepare the villagers to resist the judge, and to organise a rehearsal with himself as questioner and Mengo playing the part of the victim (ironically, Esteban himself is the first villager to be tortured by the judge). More important are the moral examples which he provides by word and deed, expressing the loyalty of the villagers to their lord (ll.549-78), firmly but courteously rebuking the Comendador for his misconduct (ll.971-1012), remaining dignified in the face of verbal and physical abuse, and condemning Fernán Gómez in the discussion with Juan Rojo, an old friend whose views match his own (ll.1317-50). At the start of Act II, Esteban's attack on astrologers who claim to find out secrets known only to God (ll.868-91) might seem an irrelevance, but in fact gives an impression of him as a pious and sensible man which is amply borne out by his conduct throughout the rest of the play.

The role of Mengo the shepherd is a challenging one: he is fat (ll.2236-37), often naive, and provides light relief with his frequently rustic and incorrect speech, his largely unjustified pride in his talent as a versifier, and his obsession with the state of his backside after his flogging; in his unaffected way he even gives the king and queen full details of this (ll.2414-33; see also ll.1643-51). However, there is another facet to his character: though illiterate he is neither stupid nor unreceptive to ideas, and argues forcefully in the debate on love that it is pure self-interest which rules the universe, and that 'nadie tiene amor/ más que a su misma persona' (ll.401-02). Whether this is a sincere belief or a mere pose taken up for the sake of argument, Mengo quickly abandons it when faced with the practical need to defend Jacinta. He emerges as a serious-minded character in this scene, and his pleas for mercy for the girl and himself (ll.1223-30, 1247-48) and his invocation of divine justice (ll.1251-52) are undoubtedly moving.

Mengo's flogging makes him understandably reluctant to take

action when the wedding is interrupted; attending the *junta* as representative of the humbler peasants (which suggests that he is a respected person in the community), he urges caution in their name, since they have suffered more than the other villagers because of Fernán Gómez and do not wish him to be provoked (ll.1703-07). Laurencia's appeal, though, moves Mengo as much as Jacinta's had done, and he is soon pressing for violent action (ll.1805-08) and hunting down Flores and Ortuño. His well-known dread of pain makes Laurencia and Frondoso fear that he will not be able to resist torture, but in fact he stands firm, though his exaggerated moans and groans afterwards are undeniably comic. Mengo the *gracioso* is thus by no means a buffoon: he is as worthy and admirable as any of the other villagers, and what makes him amusing is largely the way in which he expresses himself.

Barrildo, the friend of Mengo and Frondoso, has a small part which nonetheless contains some important lines. It is he who rebuts Mengo's views that the world is a place of 'discordia eterna' (l.374):

> El mundo de acá y de allá,
> Mengo, todo es armonía.
> Armonía es puro amor,
> porque el amor es concierto. (ll.379-82)

Barrildo has also heard of Plato, and affirms that ideally love is a spiritual thing, transcending mere physical gratification (ll.421-26). In the second act, just after Esteban's commonsense attack on astrology, Barrildo himself provides an example of the shrewdness of the countryman when he discusses the art of printing with Leonelo, and shows an openminded willingness to move with the times in his defence of an invention which the apparently cynical and blasé student condemns.[45] Loyal to his friends and to the rest of the village, Barrildo is present at the *junta*, takes part in the attack on the Comendador's house and, with Frondoso and one of the *regidores*, tends Mengo after his

[45] Ribbans (*31*, p.155) sees Leonelo as an absurd figure compared with the villagers.

interrogation.

Pascuala in many ways resembles Laurencia, being the same type of strong-willed, moral woman; like her she is suspicious of all men, thanks to Fernán Gómez (ll.249-72); she is courageous enough to stand up to the Comendador when he tries to persuade her and Laurencia to enter his house (ll.603-04), and at the wedding twice intervenes to defend Frondoso (ll.1590, 1593-94), and then again to condemn the beating of Esteban (l.1636). Her courage in the fight in Act III is matched by her defiance of the judge when he has her tortured. Jacinta is of the same sort: hers is a very small part but she also has some good lines. The important distinction between moral honour, the prerogative of the humblest citizen, and formal honour derived from mere rank and the accident of birth, is well expressed by her as she asks Fernán Gómez to respect her family's good name:

> ....tengo un padre honrado,
> que si en alto nacimiento
> no te iguala, en las costumbres
> te vence. (ll.1260-63)

The Reyes Católicos

As the villagers' *coplas* and other displays of affection show, they are a much-liked king and queen, ruling two countries united by their marriage, and themselves united by their mutual love (ll.2290-93); in this last respect they resemble Laurencia and Frondoso.[46] Fernando tends to take the lead in matters of government, but there is nonetheless a sense of shared responsibility: Isabel, for instance, has important points to make about the problems posed by Afonso of Portugal (ll.635-42) and the loss of Ciudad Real (ll.699-706); Fernando praises the skill with which she settles the affairs of Castile (ll.2298-2301), and proposes that she should judge the villagers of Fuenteovejuna, although she prefers to leave this to him (ll.2350-57). Lope

---

[46] López Estrada remarks (*21*, p.528) that the expression 'en uno' is used three times of the two village lovers (ll.738, 1297-98, 1545) and once, by Frondoso, of the Reyes (ll.2036-37).

presents them as conscientious and efficient rulers, quick to settle
the problems which confront the state, and anxious to govern
justly. Under God their task is to restore that social harmony
which is part of the divine plan for the universe, and which was
upset through the misconduct of the Comendador. The humble
village *regidor* or alderman who wishes only to 'gobernar en paz'
(l.866) also expresses unwittingly the ambition of his king and
queen. Isabel towards the end of the play leaves Castile 'en paz,
queda, quieta y llana' (l.2299), and key words in the speeches of
the Reyes are those with positive associations such as
'reformación', 'reformar', 'acuerdo', 'buen fin', 'buen suceso',
'seguro', 'asegurar', 'remediar', 'el bien del Reino'. The contrast
between the Reyes and Fernán Gómez thus reflects the traditional
belief that the rule of a good monarch was the best form of
government and that of a tyrant the worst.

In *Fuenteovejuna* Lope presents his public with a range of
characters from different social classes who display different
attitudes to life. The play revolves essentially around a clearly-
defined conflict between good and evil, but the more complex
personalities of the Maestre and Mengo suggest that Lope is
aware that this conflict can take place within the individual as well
as between opposing factions. This is a notion much developed
later by Calderón. Fernán Gómez is a total villain, but the various
forms which his villainy takes combine with the progressive
revelation of the extent of his wickedness to make him interesting.
The villagers have much in common one with another, but the
more prominent members of the community at least are
sufficiently individualized for them to be more than just a gallery
of undifferentiated rustic types, despite the growing sense of
communal solidarity and the gradual formation of the idea of the
collective protagonist. Laurencia, particularly, is a strong and
distinctive personality, and the main plot must be seen very much
in terms of her personal struggle against the Comendador, a
struggle in which the other villagers, beginning with Frondoso,
become progressively involved. Lope's characters may not be
models of psychological realism as we understand it today, but

that is hardly the point; in moral and dramatic terms they are highly impressive, and provide challenging roles for the actors as well as moving and exciting entertainment for the audience.

5 *Style and Versification*

Symbolism and Imagery

As was seen in Chapter 3, *Fuenteovejuna* possesses a high degree of structural and thematic unity: events and the themes which they embody are linked by clear patterns of association and contrast. The play's unity is further enhanced by certain recurring key words of which instances were given in Chapter 4: thus the Comendador is seen in terms of barbarism, paganism, perversity, disorder, whereas the villagers and the Reyes are associated with religion, harmony and love. Other unifying elements which need to be considered include the various references to the Cross of Calatrava and to the standard and arms of the Reyes, and Lope's frequent use of animal imagery, especially imagery connected with hunting.

Throughout the play the Comendador and Maestre wear on their chests the red cross which is the emblem of their Order, a constant reminder of the Christian ideals which they are betraying. For Fernán Gómez the cross stands instead for purely external and worldly values: courtesy, for instance, in the narrow sense of the formal politeness which one member of the Order owes another (ll.32-36; see also ll.60-64), and a superficial notion of honour as mere social standing, the prerogative of men such as himself and something from which the villagers are excluded (ll.984-88). The red colour of the cross, which should symbolize willingness to fight for the Christian faith and in defence of the poor and weak, becomes for the Comendador and the Maestre a justification for violence and bloodshed in any cause as a means of gaining worldly renown (ll.117-20, 129-40, 153-56).[47]

In Act I the Comendador is at the height of his power, dominating the villagers, fomenting rebellion against the state

---

[47] On the symbolism of the Cross of Calatrava see also *13*, pp.178 and 181, and *36*, p.18.

and capturing Ciudad Real; he, the Maestre and Flores refer to the Cross of Calatrava seven times between them, on each occasion in a proud or triumphant manner.[48] However, at the end of Act I Fernán Gómez is beginning to encounter the resistance which will finally overcome him: the Reyes are planning the recapture of Ciudad Real and Frondoso saves Laurencia from him. In the final scene Frondoso and Laurencia remind him of the Christian values which the cross represents (ll.810-13, 825-29); the eventual triumph of these values is suggested in a striking tableau by Frondoso's use of the crossbow to thwart the Comendador as the act closes (see *36*, pp.24-25).

During the second act the Comendador's position is deteriorating: Frondoso's defiance has clearly unsettled him (see ll.1044-48), Ciudad Real is retaken by the royal army, and his vengeful kidnapping of Laurencia and Frondoso leads only to his overthrow and death in Act III. It is appropriate that references to the emblem which for him symbolizes temporal power and glory should now be fewer and linked with the ideas of unworthiness and defeat. When, early in Act II, Fernán Gómez boasts of his aristocratic honour which the villagers cannot share ('¿Vosotros honor tenéis?/ ¡Qué freiles de Calatrava!' (ll.987-88)), the Regidor informs him that the mere wearing of a badge does not make a man honourable in any meaningful sense:

> Alguno acaso se alaba
> de la Cruz que le ponéis,
> que no es de sangre tan limpia. (ll.989-91)[49]

The same point is made by Esteban at the end of Act II, when he speaks of the imminent victory of Fernando and Isabel over the forces of disorder:

---

[48] Flores, it will be recalled, suggests to the villagers (ll.457-68 and 517-20) that the capture of Ciudad Real was a Christian victory over the infidel and thus in keeping with the Order's aims.

[49] The question of honour and *limpieza de sangre* is considered more fully below in Chapter 6.

Y harán mal, cuando descansen
de las guerras, en sufrir
en sus villas y lugares
a hombres tan poderosos
por traer cruces tan grandes.
Póngasela el Rey al pecho,
que para pechos reales
es esa insignia, y no más. (ll.1623-30)

In Act III Flores tells the Reyes of the humiliating end of Fernán Gómez and the wounds inflicted on his 'cruzado pecho' (l.1978). Finally the submission of the Calatravans to the royal authority is shown in the repentant Maestre's plea for forgiveness and his promise henceforth to use the forces of the order for their intended purpose of defending the faith, and not for personal aggrandizement:

...en aquesta jornada
de Granada, adonde vais,
os prometo que veáis
el valor que hay en mi espada;
donde, sacándola apenas,
dándoles fieras congojas,
plantaré mis cruces rojas
sobre sus altas almenas. (ll.2326-33)

A symbol which acquires increasing importance as the fortunes of Fernán Gómez and the Calatravans decline is the banner of the Reyes Católicos, representing the unity of Christian Spain. In Act II Cimbranos describes how the Maestre and his men, besieged in Ciudad Real, see the torches and flags of the royal army approaching:

Ya divisan con las luces
desde las altas almenas,
los castillos y leones
y barras aragonesas. (ll.1117-20)

Later, having failed to hold the town, the Comendador and Maestre flee with the 'pendón de Calatrava' (l.1454) which is all that they have saved. Triumphant shouts of '¡Vitoria por los reyes de Castilla!' are heard from off stage (l.1459) as the Maestre looks back and sees how:

> Ya coronan de luces las almenas,
> y las ventanas de las torres altas
> entoldan con pendones vitoriosos. (ll.1460-62)

There is an echo of this scene when in Act III the villagers set off under their improvised banners (ll.1801-03, 1837-43) to attack the Comendador's house, shouting in support of Fernando and Isabel. After their victory they deface the Comendador's carved coat of arms above the entrance and plan to set up instead the arms of the Reyes (ll.1992-94). The villagers' identification with the royal cause is shown vividly when Juan Rojo brings in a shield bearing the royal arms and displays it amidst general rejoicing:

ESTEBAN: ¡Bravo escudo!
BARRILDO: ¡Qué contento!
FRONDOSO: Ya comienza a amanecer
                        con este sol nuestro día.
ESTEBAN: ¡Vivan Castilla y León,
                        y las barras de Aragón,
                        y muera la tiranía! (ll.2075-80)

As is common in Golden Age drama, the forces of good are here identified with light and the sun, and those of evil with darkness and night (see also ll.1117 and 1460, cited above). Having opposed evil separately during the play, the Reyes and the villagers are at last brought together in the final scene, and the unifying symbol of the royal arms is mentioned again:

ESTEBAN: Señor, tuyos ser queremos.
                        Rey nuestro eres natural,
                        y con título de tal

ya tus armas puesto habemos.

(ll.2434-37)

Images connected with hunting and with the slaughter of animals are frequent in *Fuenteovejuna*, and relate to the Comendador's cruelty and more especially to his voracious sexual appetites. An early example is Laurencia's remark that though only a young chicken or 'polla', she is too tough for the Comendador — as turns out, of course, to be the case (ll.215-16). A little later she likens Flores, the Comendador's pimp, to a hunter's hawk (l.447), and Ortuño suggests that, like the villagers' gift of food, Laurencia and Pascuala are just so much flesh to be provided for his master's pleasure (ll.619-25). In his first words to Laurencia Fernán Gómez had called her 'hermosa fiera' (l.601), and the image of the hunt of love is much developed in the final scene of Act I when he confronts her while he is actually out hunting deer and refers to her as 'bella gama' and 'caza' (ll.781, 836). As Gerli points out, 'the whole episode is reminiscent of numerous ballads utilizing the hunt as an allegory of courtship' (*10*, p.55).[50] An ironic reversal of the situation ends this incident as Frondoso menaces the Comendador with his own bow, turning the hunter into the hunted.

The hawk and the deer often have erotic associations in traditional Hispanic ballads and lyric poetry; the same is true of the hare, and early in Act II Fernán Gómez mockingly asks for the aid of Esteban's swift hound in catching 'una liebre que por pies/ por momentos se me va' (ll.959-60), meaning Laurencia.[51] As this act progresses and the Comendador's conduct becomes more villainous, he is seen as a wild beast of prey rather than as a human hunter — 'sangrienta fiera' (l.1148) and 'tigre' (l.1184). He pursues Laurencia with 'linces deseos' (ll.1556, 1568). When Mengo tries to defend Jacinta with his sling the audience thinks

[50] See also *13*, p.180. Such imagery is a commonplace of European literature: see Marcelle Thiébaux, *The Stag of Love: The Chase in Medieval Literature* (Ithaca: Cornell University Press, 1974).

[51] See Raymond E. Barbera, 'An Instance of Medieval Iconography in *Fuenteovejuna*', *Romance Notes*, 10 (1968-69), 160-62.

perhaps of David and Goliath but also of how the shepherd must defend his flock against wolves; the image becomes explicit in Act III when Laurencia rebukes the village men for not daring to prevent her own abduction:

> Llevóme de vuestros ojos
> a su casa Fernán Gómez;
> la oveja al lobo dejáis
> como cobardes pastores. (ll.1740-43)[52]

She then condemns the men as timid sheep themselves (ll.1758-59), as cowardly hares (l.1768), and as chickens (ll.1770-71). Laurencia would rather the men displayed the qualities of tigers who '...feroces/ siguen quien roba sus hijos,/ matando los cazadores' (ll.1763-65). When she does finally goad them into acting there is a second ironic reversal and the hunter becomes the hunted once again as the Comendador is brought to bay and killed.

Other instances of animal imagery include such brief and highly conventional examples as 'perro' and 'caballo' for insults (ll.830 and 2211; 1.1634) and the Comendador's description of his followers as like lions for bravery (l.161). More interesting is Pascuala's lengthy comparison of men with the fickle and ungrateful sparrow (ll.249-72); this contrasts with Frondoso's image of the doves, traditionally representing peace and affection, to describe the happy marriage with Laurencia for which he longs: '...ambos como palomos/ estemos, juntos los picos,/ con arrullos sonorosos' (ll.768-70).

Levels of style

Lope was aware that factors such as differences of social background are reflected in the way in which people speak.[53] Nevertheless, the villagers in *Fuenteovejuna* often express themselves in a comparatively elevated and cultured manner which might be seen as completely unsuited to their origins. It

---

[52] There is a clearer religious allusion here as well: see St John, ch.10, vv.11-12.

[53] See *Arte nuevo*, ll.269-88; *1*, pp.132-33.

can be considered appropriate enough, however, if one bears in
mind Lope's concept, shared at least in theory by so many of his
contemporaries, of the moral superiority of the countryman;
this emerges in the peasants' various discourses on philosophical, legal and ethical questions, expressed in what López
Estrada calls 'un vocabulario humanístico, de intención culta y
jurídica' (*21*, p.523). When the scene moves from the Maestre's
residence to the village early in Act I, Lope inserts a number of
examples of archaic and rustic usage into the initial dialogue
between Pascuala and Laurencia in which the girls condemn the
lasciviousness of Fernán Gómez and exalt a life of simplicity and
virtue (ll.173-274). Instances include 'a la he' (l.174), 'brando'
(l.182), 'voto al sol' (l.187), the realistic details of Laurencia's
description of her daily routine (ll.215-48), simple imagery
derived from rural life (ll.181-82, 183-84, 249-72), and a typical
proverb or *refrán* (ll.185-86). The effect of these is to emphasize
the change of scene and the differences in manners and morals
between *aldea* and *corte* which are so important throughout the
play. With the arrival of Frondoso, Barrildo and Mengo and the
debate on morality, harmony and love (ll.275-444), the speech of
the villagers becomes more learned, and technical terms and
abstract ideas abound. There are only a few examples of peasant
or colloquial speech to remind the audience that this is a
discussion between country people: 'dimuño' (l.349), 'soncas'
(l.350), 'cademia' (l.430), 'quistión' (l.437). Other instances
occur when the villagers greet the Comendador after Flores's
heroic account of the taking of Ciudad Real: 'Comendadore'
(l.530), 'vencedore' (l.540), 'vueso' (l.559); the *aldea-corte*
contrast is further emphasized here by Alonso's juxtaposition of
'espadaña' and 'juncia' (ll.583-84), suggesting rural simplicity,
and 'perlas orientales' (l.585), indicative of aristocratic luxury.[54]
Shortly afterwards, Laurencia and Pascuala use such
expressions as '¡tirte ahuera!' (l.600), 'harre' (l.613) and 'vueso'
(l.623) in their argument with Fernán Gómez and his *criados*

---

[54] Note also that in this passage the villagers are associated with animals
connected with peaceful husbandry (capons, hens, geese, for example) whereas a
little earlier the Comendador and Maestre had been linked with their horses,
animals connected with the *caballero*'s traditional activities of hunting and
especially war (ll.469-88).

who try to lure them into the Comendador's house; in this way, as López Estrada notes (*21*, p.523), they distance themselves socially from the immoral *hidalgo* who is seeking to seduce them.

During the remainder of the play the villagers for the most part make only occasional use of the kind of archaic or rustic language cited above.[55] Mengo, who is one of the lowest in the social scale, is particularly given to such expressions. His speech is comically quaint and earthy, as is seen in his *coplas* (ll.1503-09 and 2061-67), his comparison of poets with *buñoleros* (ll.1514-33), and his description of his backside after the flogging as resembling a slice of salmon (ll.1650, 2424-25).

Whereas the speech of the villagers tends to become more refined as the play proceeds, the reverse is true in the case of the Comendador. In the opening scene his speech reveals, despite his impatience, the elevated style expected of an *hidalgo*. It is distinguished by *sentencias*, metaphorical language, and abstract ideas:

> Conquistará poco amor.
> Es llave la cortesía
> para abrir la voluntad;
> y para la enemistad,
> la necia descortesía. (ll.12-16)

There is an obvious contrast with the more down-to-earth manner of the *criado* Ortuño, who prefers to talk in terms of concrete examples rather than generalities:

> Si supiese un descortés
> cómo lo aborrecen todos,
> y querrían de mil modos
> poner la boca a sus pies,
> antes que serlo ninguno,
> se dejaría morir. (ll.17-22)

---

[55] Thus we find 'vusiñoría' (ll.941 and 949), 'quistión' (l.956), 'alimpia' (l.994), 'voto al sol' (ll.1169 and 1214), 'soceso' (l.1224), 'ascondes' (ll.1554 and 1556), 'respingo' (l.2064), 'agora' (ll.2065 and 2098), 'cagajón' (l.2112).

In his rhetorical harangue to the Maestre, Fernán Gómez speaks
in a suitably heroic manner, developing at length the symbol of
the red Cross of Calatrava (ll.129-40), and giving his speech a
sophisticated and classical ring through the use of such
expressions as 'la fama' (l.123), 'los laureles' (l.124), 'las alas de
la fama' (l.127), and 'templo inmortal/ de vuestros claros
pasados' (ll.139-40). During the rest of the play, however, his
style is very different, and shows none of the *cortesía* to which
he pays lip-service. There is the occasional *cultismo*, such as his
remark on the losses suffered by the royal army ('A fe, que es
más tragedia que no fiesta', l.1464), but more commonly his
speeches, terse and abrupt, are characterized by oaths, threats,
curses, mockery, sarcasm, peremptory orders and insults; these
last, as we have seen, often involve the scornful use of animal
imagery. The differences between the Comendador's style and
that of the villagers further emphasize the moral gulf between
them: when Jacinta is abducted, for instance, her pleas for
mercy involve the use of abstract concepts and legal terminology
('Apelo de tu crueldad/ a la justicia divina', ll.1275-76), as well
as metaphorical language:

> ...tengo un padre honrado,
> que si en alto nacimiento
> no te iguala, en las costumbres
> te vence. (ll.1260-63)

These offer a strong contrast with such remarks of Fernán
Gómez as '¡tira por ahí' (l.1266), 'Ya no mía, del bagaje/ del
ejército has de ser' (ll.1269-70), 'Ea, villana, camina' (l.1273),
and 'No hay piedad' (l.1274).

Irony and wit

The action of *Fuenteovejuna* is for the most part serious, and
what humour there is tends to be verbal, as in Mengo's speeches
with their comic mispronunciations (ll.1175, 2066-67) and
diminutives (l.2249) and the rustic usages mentioned above. A
good deal of this verbal humour results from irony, as when a

character's words have a significance which he fails to see but is perceived by the audience, or when what he says has a hidden meaning for himself but which other characters miss. Unconscious irony of the first sort is something to which the villains of Golden Age plays are peculiarly prone. An example of unconscious irony occurs when Fernán Gómez expresses his willingness to fight Frondoso, despite the convention that an *hidalgo* should not duel with a social inferior: his words 'guárdate, que rompo/ las leyes de caballero' (ll.849-50) are an unintentional admission of his failure to live up to far more important and fundamental aspects of his position in society. Similar instances occur when the Comendador makes statements which the audience knows to be at variance with the facts, as in his dismissal of the villagers as unwarlike (ll.162-65), or when he accuses others of faults which he displays himself; examples include his denunciation of the Maestre's lack of courtesy in the opening scene of Act I, his calling Laurencia a monster (ll.786-90), and his condemnation of Frondoso as a rebel who deserves to be punished (ll.1596-1606). Esteban the *alcalde* is perhaps being unintentionally ironical when he describes to Fernán Gómez the tribute of food which the village has presented to him; certainly his reference to the geese 'que sacan por las redes las cabezas,/ para cantar vueso valor guerrero' (ll.558-59) is a touch of bathos which makes the Comendador and his exploits seem rather ridiculous. Conscious irony, which the audience notices but the Comendador fails to see, occurs when Flores remarks that discourtesy to a social inferior is akin to tyranny (ll.25-28), and possibly when Ortuño says how the discourteous are universally detested (ll.17-22).

Verbal humour can be found also in the *conceptos* or puns which appear at intervals. Some reflect merely the vulgar or mocking spirit of the Comendador and his followers (e.g. ll.625, 969-70), but the majority are expressions of the villagers' cheerful good nature. Mengo, for instance, explains Laurencia's intelligence or wit ('sal') by remarking that the priest must have used too much salt when christening her (ll.351-52), and she shows her wit a moment afterwards in her pun on the expression 'prestar oído' (ll.356-58); Esteban jokingly remarks (ll.569-74)

that with some skins of wine ('cueros') available, a soldier can
defy the coldest weather even if naked ('en cueros'), and the
student Leonelo plays on the words 'Bártulo' (a member of the
Colegio de San Bartolomé at Salamanca)[56] and 'barbero'
(l.895). The villagers' sense of triumph and relief when the judge
abandons his investigation leads Frondoso to place a humorous
interpretation on Mengo's groans of pain — which may themselves be amusingly exaggerated (l.2274); a little later Frondoso
and Laurencia comically re-enact the judge's failure to obtain
confessions, and play on the notions of being actually killed and
dying metaphorically of love (ll.2288-89). Blacker humour is
found in Mengo's observation that anyone wishing to see
cardinals need not go to Rome but merely glance at the red weals
('cardenales') across his back (ll.1644-46). This, together with
Laurencia's pun on 'voto' and 'voces' when she interrupts the
council meeting (l.1715), should serve to remind modern readers
and audiences that Lope and his contemporaries saw nothing
out of place in using wit and word-play in serious or even tragic
situations.

Versification

The versification of *Fuenteovejuna* presents few problems:[57]
generally speaking, the use of different metres in different
situations is in agreement with Lope's own observations on the
subject:

> Acomode los versos con prudencia
> a los sujetos de que va tratando;
> las décimas son buenas para quejas,
> el soneto está bien en los que aguardan,
> las relaciones piden los romances
> aunque en otavas lucen por extremo,
> son los tercetos para cosas graves,

---

[56] Or possibly a lawyer, after the famous Italian jurist of the early fourteenth
century, Bartolo de Sassoferrato. Either way, a person of academic distinction.

[57] For an analysis of the verse-forms used in the play see for example *3*, pp.25-
28.

y para las de amor las redondillas.
(*Arte nuevo*, ll.305-12; *1*, pp.133-34)

Of the metres which Lope mentions, *décimas* (lines of eight
syllables in strophes of ten lines having a varying rhyme scheme)
are not used in *Fuenteovejuna* at all; the reason would appear to
lie in Lope's recommendation of them for 'quejas', the
anguished pleas of unhappy lovers declaring feelings which are
not reciprocated. *Décimas* would hardly be appropriate for
Frondoso's courtship of Laurencia: despite her suspicion of
men, she is much aware of his good looks and elegant bearing
(ll.731-34), and they think alike on important subjects as their
dialogue on sincerity and hypocrisy shows (ll.290-348). As soon
as he proposes marriage she is inclined to accept (ll.772-74), and
when he defends her against Fernán Gómez her reaction is one
of gratitude and love. Their love is mutual, and the obstacles to
their happiness are the purely external threats posed by the lust
of the Comendador and the judge's investigations.

It is perhaps the stricter form and the concision of the sonnet
which make it appropriate for soliloquies in which, at moments
of crisis, characters speak gravely but tersely of their hopes or
fears as they await the outcome of events. The only sonnet in
Fuenteovejuna is Laurencia's speech (ll.2161-74) describing her
concern for Frondoso just before the judge begins to question
the villagers. The sonnet is divided into four short, self-
contained sections; tension increases as the two quatrains,
relating in general terms the suffering caused by fear for a loved
one, give way to the two briefer tercets, on Laurencia's specific
fear for Frondoso's safety.

Romance can have any number of lines; they are of eight
syllables, and instead of rhyme there is an assonanced ending to
the second line of each couplet. It is the popular Spanish ballad
metre, and tends to have warlike and heroic associations;
romantic and sentimental ballads are common enough, but
many others — whether deriving from epics or based on more
recent historical events — relate the courageous deeds of knights
and champions. Originally a form of oral literature, *romances* did

not disappear with the invention of printing: they continued to circulate orally (in many cases down to our own times), while the reading public purchased collections or anthologies of traditional ballads, which also circulated — often in shortened form — in cheap, popular *pliegos sueltos* or chap-books; poets such as Quevedo, Góngora and Lope himself produced, though in a more sophisticated style, ballads of their own.[58] The continuing popularity of the form, which was enjoyed by Spaniards of all classes, can be seen in the extent to which seventeenth-century dramatists use *romance* in their plays: nearly thirty per cent of *Fuenteovejuna* is in this metre. Since it can be of any length and dispenses with full rhyme, *romance* has something of the freedom and naturalness of prose; this makes it ideally suited to long narrative passages or 'relaciones', and it is very often used to relate background historical information or — for instance by envoys or messengers — to describe battles and campaigns. Examples in *Fuenteovejuna* are numerous: the Comendador employs *romance* to inform the Maestre of Afonso's claim to the throne of Castile before urging him to support the pretender (ll.69-140); it is in this metre that Flores describes both the taking of Ciudad Real (ll.457-528) and his master's death (ll.1948-2013); the *regidores* of Ciudad Real use *romance* to tell the Reyes of the loss of their town (ll.655-98), Cimbranos reports the approach of the royal army in *romance* (ll.1105-27), and Laurencia uses it to recount her sufferings and Frondoso's danger (ll.1712-93). *Romance* is thus linked above all with violence and the misdeeds of the Comendador; the same is true on the occasions when it is used not in monologue but in dialogue, as when Frondoso's wooing of Laurencia is interrupted by Fernán Gómez at the end of Act I, and when the Comendador arrives to break up their wedding at the end of Act II. On the latter occasion his appearance is preceded by a song, partly in *romance* metre, which relates his previous attempt at seducing her (ll.1546-69).[59] It was in a variant of *romance*, with

---

[58] See *Studies of the Spanish and Portuguese Ballad*, ed. N.D. Shergold (London: Tamesis, 1972).

[59] There is an *estribillo* or refrain (ll.1554-57 and 1566-69) in *seguidillas*, with

six-syllable lines, that the villagers had earlier sung his praises when he returned from capturing Ciudad Real (ll.529-44 and 591-94).

Octavas reales have eleven-syllable lines arranged in eight-line strophes rhyming ABABABCC; Lope considered this metre to be very appropriate for 'relaciones', and it appears in the opening scene of Act II in which Esteban attacks astrologers and Leonelo gives an account of the invention of printing and its consequences. Such weighty issues find suitable expression in the formal, rather stately *octavas reales*; they are also employed for the climax of the villagers' revolt and the Comendador's death (ll.1848-1919), and the gravity of the metre befits the occasion.

Tercetos also have lines of eleven syllables; the rhyme scheme can vary slightly: Lope gives us, for instance, ABA BCB CDC DED when the metre is first brought in at l.545, but when it reappears at the start of Act III (l.1652) we find ABA BCB DCD EDE. Like the sonnet and the *octava real*, the *terceto* is a *culto* rather than a popular metre; Lope recommended it for 'cosas graves', and in *Fuenteovejuna* he uses it for the villagers' welcoming of the Comendador (ll.545-78), a ceremony which is intended to be serious and formal, even though Esteban's speech is not quite up to the occasion. In Act III the meeting of the village *junta* (ll.1652-1711) is in *tercetos* up to the arrival of Laurencia; the metre is in keeping with the mood of crisis as Esteban and the *regidor* denounce Fernán Gómez and the *regidor* goes on to make the awesome proposal that they should rise up against him and his men.

Just under sixty per cent of *Fuenteovejuna* is written in *redondillas*; these have lines of eight syllables, arranged in quatrains rhyming ABBA. Lope felt that this sprightly metre was appropriate to 'cosas de amor', and we find it in cheerful, lively scenes where marriage is proposed and the details of weddings arranged (see e.g. ll.1277-1448), and also in the vigorous and fast-moving debate on love (ll.275-444). The predominance of *redondillas* throughout the play underlines the importance in

couplets of seven and five syllables and assonanced endings on the second line of each couplet.

Fuenteovejuna of the theme of true love (whether sexual attraction or loyal friendship) as opposed to lust, selfishness and violence. Casalduero noted how often Lope reminds us of the conflict by juxtaposing passages in *redondillas* with others in *romance* (*8*, passim). Thus in Act I the debate on love in *redondillas* is followed by Flores's account in *romance* of the capture of Ciudad Real and the massacre in the town. When the Reyes first appear they talk in *redondillas*, which is perhaps Lope's way of stressing that these rulers of a united Spain are united in love as well (ll.635-54); the *regidores* of Ciudad Real make their report in *romance*, and the scene closes with the king and queen, in *redondillas*, making the necessary plans to deal with the rebellion and re-impose their authority (ll.699-722). Similarly, in Act III, the recapture of Ciudad Real and the consequent weakening of Afonso's cause are described in *redondillas* (ll.1920-47) immediately prior to Flores's arrival to announce in *romance* the death of Fernán Gómez. Apart from the villagers' *coplas* praising the Reyes, and Laurencia's sonnet, the remainder of Act III is in *redondillas*, perhaps indicative of the ultimate triumph of love as represented by the king and queen and the people of Fuenteovejuna.

Redondillas are not found exclusively in scenes involving the Reyes and the villagers where the idea of true love is more or less explicit; Lope employs them, for instance, in a dialogue in Act II between Fernán Gómez, Flores and Ortuño (ll.1023-1102). This may be an ironical way of reminding the audience through implication of the existence of true love as the Comendador discusses his squalid erotic escapades with the *criados* who pimp for him. It is harder to see what, if any, is the point of using *redondillas* in the first scene of Act I before and after the Comendador's harangue to the Maestre in *romance* metre (ll.1-68 and 141-72). Would members of a Golden Age audience have been shocked and startled at the spectacle of a meeting of rebels and traitors expressed in a metre more commonly associated with courtship and love? Is this a discrepancy deliberately intended to relate to the chaos and disorder which Fernán Gómez wreaks on so many levels throughout much of the play? Perhaps Lope is implying nothing, for he did use *redondillas* for ordinary dialogue,[60] and his choice of them here could simply have been on the grounds of their being suited to the short, rapid exchanges of this tense opening scene.

Versos sueltos, not mentioned by Lope in the *Arte nuevo*, are used for the scene in Act II in which Fernán Gómez and the Maestre are defeated at Ciudad Real (ll.1449-71); the lines are mostly of eleven syllables but with some of twelve, and there is a mixture of blank verse and rhyme. The effect of confusion is appropriate to the situation in which the rebels find themselves, uncertain how to react (ll.1466-68) following their defeat by the royal army. Here as elsewhere Lope's craftsmanship can be seen in his selection of verse-forms 'contributing definable, if variable, meanings to the dramatic content...valid clues to the dramatic meaning'.[61]

[60] Marín (*24*, pp.12-21) maintains that after about 1615 Lope tended to do this more often.

[61] J.W. Sage, *Lope de Vega, 'El caballero de Olmedo'*, Critical Guides to Spanish Texts, 6 (London: Grant and Cutler, 1974), p.74.

6 *Themes*

Town and Country

Like many other Golden Age *comedias*, *Fuenteovejuna* presents
a picture of idealized country life (*aldea*) together with more or
less explicit criticism of the court and the town (*corte*). To some
extent this reflects the audience's desire for novelty and contrast:
dramatists such as Lope wrote for audiences of nobles and
townsfolk seeking to escape for a while from their everyday lives
(see *32*, p.915). A related point, stressed by Varey, is the fact
that Madrid, where Lope lived and worked for most of his life,
was a new city which had grown rapidly and where many of the
population were only first- or second-generation city-dwellers;
the principal source of entertainment was the theatre, and
dramatists catered for a certain nostalgia for the countryside in
their portrayal of an idyllic rural world free from the pressures
and problems of urban life, and ultimately triumphant over
whatever external forces might threaten it.[62] In reality,
conditions were frequently harsh for the peasant farmers and
labourers who made up the bulk of Spain's predominantly rural
population: seigneurial dues, Church tithes and taxes to the
Crown combined with primitive farming methods and scanty or
uncertain harvests to produce a generally low standard of living;
plague and inflation were additional causes of suffering and
demoralization.[63] Poverty and debt drove many peasants to the
towns in the early seventeenth century and it is strange, given the
misery from which they had fled, that the *comedia* should
idealize village life. However, even when home has been

[62] J.E. Varey, 'The Essential Ambiguity in Lope de Vega's *Peribáñez*: Theme
and Staging', *Theatre Research International*, new series, 1 (1976), 157-78, at
p.157.

[63] For the conditions in the countryside in the early seventeenth century see, for
instance, John Lynch, *Spain under the Habsburgs*, 2nd edition (Oxford: Basil
Blackwell, 1981), II, pp.1-8.

abandoned for good reasons, exiles and their descendants often look back on it nostalgically. R.O. Jones has suggested that in an era of increasing economic decline the peasant was seen as being the possible saviour of an overwhelmingly agricultural society,[64] while Salomon uses the expression 'propaganda for a return to the land' of plays such as *Fuenteovejuna* (*32*, p.914), but we have no means of telling whether Lope really wrote in the hope that some of his audience might be persuaded by his plays to return to the countryside. The prosperity of the villagers of Fuenteovejuna might tempt one to conclude that Lope is implying a contrast between the Spain of his time and a bygone age of abundance, but again there is no definite proof that he intended anything of the sort.

The theme of dispraise of the city and praise of the country is also a commonplace of European culture going back to Classical times. Lope's use of it is thus a response to more general literary influences as well as to the immediate circumstances and preoccupations of his own era. In Spain from the early decades of the sixteenth century the theme appears in the works of pastoral poets and novelists, frequently inspired by Italian Renaissance authors. More realistic and considerably more moralizing is the picture of the countryside which emerges from Antonio de Guevara's *Menosprecio de corte y alabanza de aldea* (1539), an influential work which acquired a European reputation. Some consideration of Guevara is necessary here, for the *Menosprecio* helped form the concept of a moral, honourable and Christian peasantry which is central to *Fuenteovejuna* and many other Golden Age *comedias*.

Guevara sees village life as having many practical advantages over the town: it is freer and more informal, the air is purer and disease less common. In addition, food, drink and fuel are abundant and cheap. Echoes of such notions appear in Laurencia's account of her daily routine (ll.215-48) and in Esteban's description of the rich tribute of wine and provisions which the villagers are able to present to the Comendador

---

[64] 'Poets and Peasants', in *Homenaje a William L. Fichter: estudios y ensayos sobre el teatro antiguo hispánico, y otros ensayos*, ed. A. David Kossoff and José Amor y Vázquez (Madrid: Castalia, 1971), pp.341-55, at p.342.

(ll.549-78). More important, though, is the extent to which Guevara emphasizes the moral superiority of *aldea* over *corte*: in the countryside one finds true religion, a love of virtue and a hatred of vice; countrypeople judge others by their real merits rather than in accordance with such external factors as rank or wealth: 'Es privilegio del aldea que allí sea el bueno hombre honrado por bueno y el ruin conoscido por ruin, lo qual no es assí en la corte ni en las grandes repúblicas, a do ninguno es servido y acatado por lo que vale, sino por lo que tiene.'[65] Guevara sees the flattery and hypocrisy of the townsman as inverting traditional ethical values:

> En la corte todos son obispos para crismar y curas para baptizar y mudar nombres, es a saber, que al sobervio llaman honrado; al pródigo, magnífico; al cobarde, atentado; al esforçado, atrevido; al encapotado, grave; al recogido, hipócrita; al malicioso, agudo; al deslenguado, eloquente; al indeterminado, prudente; al adúltero, enamorado; al loco, regocijado; al entremetido, solícito; al chocarrero, donoso; al avaro, templado; al sospechoso, adevino, y aun al callado, bovo y nescio. (p.100)

Both López Estrada and Varey (*3*, p.55; *36*, pp.10-13) indicate the similarities between such passages in Guevara and the passage in Act I of *Fuenteovejuna* in which Laurencia and Frondoso comment on the contemporary tendency to see virtues as vices and vices as virtues (ll.290-348). There is an obvious irony in the fact that this form of *descortesía* characterizes the inhabitants of the city or *corte* (ll.321-23).

However, Lope seems aware that to identify *aldea* wholly with morality and *corte* wholly with immorality is an over-simplification. Whereas Guevara and others present the issue in black and white terms, Lope gives his audience a more complex and thus more interesting as well as more realistic picture. It is easier for the peasant, living close to nature and thus close to

---

[65] Antonio de Guevara, *Menosprecio de corte y alabanza de aldea*, ed. M. Martínez de Burgos, Clásicos Castellanos, 29 (1915; repr. Madrid: Espasa-Calpe, 1952), pp.89-90.

God, to lead a good life than it is for the townsman or courtier in his more artificial environment, but the countryside is not totally perfect and the town is not completely corrupt. Not all the village women reject the Comendador (ll.799-809 and 1064-80), and Mengo has to learn the lesson of altruism and brotherly love. The Maestre repents of his misdeeds and becomes worthy of his lineage and his position in society, while the court of the Reyes is shown throughout as a place of virtue, love and justice. Lope contrasts the conduct of the villagers with that of Fernán Gómez, but he establishes important parallels with the Reyes and Laurencia and Frondoso. The notion that morality and justice are not found solely in the countryside appears in Act II when the Comendador rejects the villagers' protests at his treatment of their womenfolk:

COMENDADOR: ¡Qué cansado villanaje!
　　　　　　 ¡Ah! Bien hayan las ciudades
　　　　　　 que a hombres de calidades
　　　　　　 no hay quien sus gustos ataje.
　　　　　　 Allá se precian casados
　　　　　　 que visiten sus mujeres.
ESTEBAN:　　 No harán, que con esto quieres
　　　　　　 que vivamos descuidados.
　　　　　　 En las ciudades hay Dios,
　　　　　　 y más presto quien castiga. (ll.999-1008)

Esteban maintains that the Comendador's account of the moral laxity of the town is exaggerated: in the town, as in the country, Christian values apply, and justice to punish the wrongdoer is more readily available. The latter point is perhaps demonstrated in Act III when the villagers have no alternative to taking the law into their own hands in order to save Frondoso's life and obtain redress against Fernán Gómez. Though on the whole he accepts the convention of the superiority of village life and respects the rural nostalgia of his audiences, Lope still shows the town to have some merits; his public, it should be remembered, were *madrileños* after all.

Honour

'Los casos de la honra', as Lope remarked in the *Arte nuevo* (ll.327-28; *1*, p.134) appealed to Spaniards of all classes. *Fuenteovejuna* is one of a number of Golden Age *comedias* in which an affair of honour involves peasants, dishonoured by *hidalgos* who desire their womenfolk, seeking redress through personal vengeance. Such a situation implies a distinction between two kinds of honour. There is the purely formal kind, the prerogative of the aristocracy, deriving from noble birth and the possession of rank and titles; in the seventeenth-century theatre aristocratic villains who have this superficial sort of honour scorn — as does Fernán Gómez (ll.987-88) — the feelings of the commoners whom they offend, forgetting that authority and privilege impose corresponding obligations towards those lower in the social scale. The second kind of honour, displayed by the usually idealized and prosperous peasant protagonists, involves such moral qualities as love, piety, hard work, patriotism and respect for the law. Whoever displays these deserves to enjoy the respect of his fellows and is reasonably entitled to feel dishonoured when his standing in the community is menaced.

The idea that a commoner has his own sense of honour and may be justified in defending it, is less daring or radical than might at first be supposed. Firstly, the peasant heroes of the *comedias* are often in fact virtually *hidalgos* in all but name, and their defence of their honour is approved by the monarch who traditionally concludes the play by praising the good and condemning the wicked. There is little here at which any *hidalgo* in a Golden Age audience could take offence, and aristocratic villains are in any case often balanced by other nobles in the *comedia* who provide examples of generous and honourable conduct.[66] In the second place, those in authority were expected

[66] The frequency with which *hidalgos* appear as the villains in peasant-honour *comedias* is clearly due to reasons of dramatic effectiveness rather than to hostility towards the nobility on the part of writers or of a section of their public. A peasant villain would have comparatively little scope for doing harm, but a more tense and intriguing situation is created when commoners are menaced by powerful aristocratic villains supported by their soldiers and retainers. Although so often idealized, the peasant heroes tend to be genuine commoners rather than

to display moderation and respect for their inferiors who were, after all, Christians and Spaniards. The belief is reflected in Mengo's appeal for mercy when the Comendador orders him to be flogged — '¡Piedad,/ piedad, pues sois hombre noble!' (ll.1247-48) — and also in Pascuala's intervention on Frondoso's behalf — 'Si os ofendió, perdonadle,/ por ser vos quien sois' (ll.1593-94). A kind of social contract seems to be implied here, and the *hidalgo* who fails to keep his side of it deserves retribution, at least in theory.[67] The concept of the honourable peasant is related furthermore to the widely-accepted notion of the superiority of *aldea* over *corte*: the distinction between moral honour which anyone may have and the outward kind which is mere social standing, is suggested by Guevara in his observation cited above that in the village a good man is 'honrado por bueno' whereas in the city or court a man is respected not for 'lo que vale' but for 'lo que tiene'. Also relevant is the Renaissance and Golden Age admiration for the 'homo novus', the prosperous and worthy commoner who by his energy and virtue has risen in the world, has overcome the disadvantages of his humble origins, and deserves to be respected as much as anyone who is born into the nobility.[68] The heroes of Lope's *Peribáñez y el Comendador de Ocaña* and Calderón's *El alcalde de Zalamea* are successful selfmade men of this kind, whose sense of honour is increased by their being *cristianos viejos*. Similarly, the village of Fuenteovejuna contains 'gente muy principal' (l.980), and the inhabitants possess *limpieza de sangre*, a quality which not all the members

hidalgos in disguise who have been raised among the peasantry through chance. See *18*, p.71, and Alexey Almasov, '*Fuenteovejuna* y el honor villanesco en el teatro de Lope de Vega', *Cuadernos Hispanoamericanos*, nos 161-62 (1963), 701-55.

[67] The *Historia de Córdoba* remarks of the fate of Fernán Gómez that 'no es mal consejo para los gobernadores y señores saber moderarse en su poder y mando, no dar rienda larga a sus robos y desafueros, contenerse en la honestidad de sus casas, sin correr las ajenas mirando'. See López Estrada, *20*, p.90 and *21*, p.534.

[68] Lazarillo de Tormes tries in vain to persuade the reader that his own life is a success story of this kind. See R. W. Truman, 'Lazarillo de Tormes and the "Homo novus" tradition', *Modern Language Review*, 64 (1969), 62-67.

of the Comendador's Order can claim (ll.989-91).[69]

References to the honour of the peasantry abound throughout *Fuenteovejuna*: the adjective 'honrado' is used of Laurencia (l.347), Frondoso (l.1413), Esteban (l.1692), Jacinta's parents (ll.1228, 1260), and an unnamed victim of the Comendador's sadism (l.1494). Laurencia refers to the village as 'esta villa honrada' (l.1791), and tells the hesitant menfolk that their passivity is unworthy of 'hombres nobles' (l.1753). She prizes her personal honour above all things (l.435). The men of the village defend their right to be considered as honourable in the argument with Fernán Gómez (ll.976-1008), and Esteban obliquely criticizes the Comendador when he states that true honour is moral virtue (ll.945-47), a point made more emphatically later by Jacinta (ll.1256-63). Frondoso feels that his honour is harmed by the Comendador's insults and his advances to Laurencia (ll.825-29 and 1362-63); he is also affronted when Esteban offers him a dowry for Laurencia: '¡Mi honor queréis agraviar!' (l.1436). The villagers' collective loss of honour and their wish to regain it and take vengeance for 'agravios' are stressed in the early scenes of Act III (ll.1662-73, 1815-35), while Mengo's defiance of the judge leads Frondoso to observe that 'Justo es que honores le den' (l.2282).

Fernán Gómez, on the other hand, denies that a peasant has any honour to lose; his inability to appreciate that the villagers disagree and will not submit forever to being dishonoured leads to his eventual downfall. He dismisses them as 'gente humilde' (l.163) and their affairs as 'cosas tan viles' (l.1217); his decision that Mengo should be flogged rather than executed stems from a wish that his men should not defile their swords with the shepherd's blood (ll.1241-43). He could never lower himself to the extent of marrying a peasant girl (ll.189-91) and indeed affirms that it is an honour for such a woman to be seduced by a man of his quality (ll.995-96). This excessive pride in the honour of being an aristocrat and a senior member of a chivalric order emerges in the opening scenes of Act I when Fernán Gómez is

[69] Few Jews lived in the countryside, and to be a peasant was a fairly safe guarantee that one had no Jewish ancestors. See R.O. Jones, 'Poets and Peasants', p.343.

offended at what he feels is a lack of courtesy on the part of the Maestre:

> Cuando no sepa mi nombre,
> ¿no le sobra el que me dan
> de Comendador mayor? (ll.7-9)

Later he is curt to the point of rudeness when he acknowledges the loyal greetings and gifts of the villagers, tributes which he clearly takes for granted as being automatically due to a man of his position (ll.579-80). The outward show of honour and the privileges of the nobleman obsess him, and he fails to recognize that such privileges imply corresponding responsibilities; in this respect he offers a complete contrast with the Reyes who never abuse their position and whose only concern is with the public good. His fury that Frondoso should have dared to defy him at the end of Act I is the motive for his subsequent vendetta against the lovers in which the rest of the village are progressively involved; Frondoso's action challenges everything which he holds dear:

> ¡Que a un capitán cuya espada
> tiemblan Córdoba y Granada,
> un labrador, un mozuelo,
> ponga una ballesta al pecho!
> El mundo se acaba, Flores. (ll.1044-48)

Fernán Gómez sees no blame attaching to himself: when he says to Frondoso 'rompo/ las leyes de caballero' (ll.849-50) he is referring not to his ungentlemanly treatment of Laurencia but to his readiness to fight Frondoso even though the aristocratic code of honour forbad a man to challenge another of a different social class. His concern with the outward forms of honour rather than its moral essence receives appropriate punishment in his undignified death, following which the villagers insult the body in traditional ways by pulling its hair and striking it across the face (ll.1984-87). They also destroy the symbol of his status as an *hidalgo* by smashing the coat of arms above the door of his house (l.1992).

The Maestre's concept of aristocratic honour is less degenerate than that of the Comendador: it involves the winning of renown through heroic deeds in battle which will make him worthy of his distinguished ancestors. Fernán Gómez plays upon this yearning for *fama* in a skilful speech in which he reminds him of the need to live up to his lineage and to silence any who may have doubts about the young man's competence as Maestre de Calatrava (ll.117-40). *Fama*, however, is not to be won in an unworthy cause, and by involving him in a rebellion against his lawful sovereigns Fernán Gómez dishonours the Maestre as effectively as he dishonours the people of Fuenteovejuna. Téllez Girón's only remedy is the painful one of humbling his pride, seeking pardon and promising amendment:

> Con vergüenza voy, mas es
> honor quien puede obligarme,
> y importa no descuidarme
> en tan honrado interés. (ll.2157-60)

Having been forgiven by Fernando and Isabel, the Maestre will devote himself to fighting in their name the Moors of Granada; his undoubted military qualities will now be directed towards winning him genuine honour and glory in the service of the church and the monarchy. Presumably many of Lope's audience would know that the Maestre kept his promise of loyalty to the cause of the Reyes Católicos, dying at the siege of Loja in 1482.

When Lope wrote *Fuenteovejuna*, the belief was gaining ground that honour and dignity were no longer the prerogative of the aristocrat: as Moir observes, 'nobility, for the seventeenth-century thinkers, was a matter of virtue rather than of social position' (*38*, p.64). The play reflects this notion of a morally honourable peasantry, but it also shows the honour of the aristocracy to be admirable provided that it is founded upon such qualities as love, piety and service to society. The Reyes, who constantly display these virtues, exemplify genuine aristocratic honour; the Maestre is misled into forfeiting his honour yet finally regains it; Fernán Gómez has only the external trappings of honour and hates to see honourable conduct in others. He is, however, an unbalanced and unrepresentative type, and it would be wrong to suppose that through him Lope was attacking the aristocracy per se. Fernán Gómez is simply one element in a varied picture of the different forms which honour takes in society and the attitudes — some good, some bad — which people demonstrate towards it.

The State and the Citizen

What may be called the political implications of the play are as uncontroversial as the way in which it presents the town-country theme and the question of honour. Although it involves a peasant rising against an aristocratic villain, *Fuenteovejuna* should not be seen as being either democratic or revolutionary in spirit, although naturally it has been interpreted as such many times since the late nineteenth century, and there have been numerous tendentious productions.[70] These frequently minimize the role of the Reyes or else distort it completely and transform them into characters as evil as the Comendador himself. If, however, we lay prejudice aside and approach the play historically, we can see that it takes for granted the idea of a hierarchical society under an absolute monarchy; it is not the common people but the sovereign who guarantees each citizen's rights and personal honour, dispensing justice as God's representative upon earth. This social structure works perfectly well as long as each citizen acts out his God-given role and performs his duties towards his sovereign and his fellow-men. This Fernán Gómez refuses to do, but the villagers show him obedience and courtesy for as long as they can; their eventual revolt is not a general rejection of the established order but the result of specific grievances inflicted by one man, and more immediately of the need to act promptly in order to save Frondoso's life. The uprising is carried out in the name of the king and queen, and the only real rebels in the play are the

---

[70] Menéndez y Pelayo in 1899 first maintained that the play, although pro-monarchic, was also 'profundamente democrático' (*26*, p.178). For radical critical interpretations see *16*, pp.452-55; for radical translations, adaptations and productions, see *17*, pp.258-64. Some are mentioned above, in the Introduction; see also note 74, below.

Comendador and the Maestre who are punished respectively by death and humiliation.

Lope stresses the Comendador's tyranny, as was seen in Chapter 4, but this only partly justifies the villagers' action. Political theorists might maintain that a tyrant could justifiably be overthrown, but they had in mind a head of state against whose misrule there was no higher temporal authority to which one might appeal. For mere peasants to turn against their local lord is a terrible thing to do, as Barrildo points out (l.1699); Juan Rojo states that they can and should appeal to the Reyes (ll.1674-79), and an alternative suggestion is that they simply abandon the village altogether (ll.1684-85). Other villagers argue for direct action against the Comendador and his henchmen, but Lope does not invite us to conclude that this is the correct step to take. The meeting of the *junta* in fact appears to have reached an impasse when the situation changes with Laurencia's announcement of Frondoso's imminent execution; the circumstances justify the uprising on this occasion but it is not implied that vassals suffering under tyrannical local rulers have an automatic right to overthrow them. The affair of Fuenteovejuna is a strictly exceptional case; the villagers are quite definitely breaking the law, they commit what the king calls a grave crime (l.2444), and the violence unleashed is shocking, even though it is a kind of poetic justice upon the villain and his followers. As Pring-Mill concludes, 'though Lope is clearly behind the villagers in the decision to kill the Comendador, he is not wholly willing to commit himself to unqualified support of revolt as a legitimate solution in such a situation' (*29*, p.29).

When the normally law-abiding villagers have to act illegally to save Frondoso's life a tense and intriguing dramatic situation results. Lope appears to be raising here the distinction between the letter of the law and its spirit. The villagers break the former in order to preserve the latter, whereas the Comendador pays lip-service to the outward forms of the law yet has no real concept of justice; this is analogous to his notions of honour or of *cortesía* which lack any moral basis. Carter points out how Fernán Gómez consciously and unconsciously twists the language of honour and of law to suit his own ends (*7*, p.323);

the play shows how easily human law can be reduced to an instrument of tyranny. Fernán Gómez is narrowly legalistic in outlook, quick to cite the law when it is to his own advantage. '¿Mías no sois?' (1.603) he asks Pascuala and Laurencia, and in a sense they are indeed his, although 'no para cosas tales' (1.604). He claims that his arrest of Frondoso is justified by Frondoso's having committed an offence against the Order of Calatrava and the Maestre; punishment is necessary, and Fernán Gómez asserts that he is acting out of an impartial desire to see justice done and not from personal spite (ll.1582-83 and 1594-1606). When Esteban protests that in defying him Frondoso was only protecting his wife, the Comendador has a ready answer: 'Nunca yo quise quitarle/ su mujer, pues no lo era' (ll.l6l7-l8); unlike her husband or a relative, a woman's suitor or fiancé was not entitled to take action against a man who offended her (see 7, p.323). Legalistically, then, Frondoso was in the wrong, notwithstanding the fact that his intervention prevented an attempt at rape. The Comendador's pretended concern for the law does not last much longer, however, and having got Frondoso in his power he is soon planning to execute him out of hand (ll.1784-87).

Like Frondoso's defence of Laurencia, the village uprising, though strictly speaking against the law, can be justified in human terms: it combines revenge for dishonour, the punishment of a rebel and tyrant, and the rescue of a man from an unjust death. The villagers' action is both right and wrong, and the difficulty of evaluating it must have intrigued Lope's audiences. King Fernando's solution respects both the letter and the spirit of the law: having heard the account of the Comendador's villainy and the villagers' assurances of loyalty (recalling the speech of the Maestre to the Reyes, ll.2310-37), he grants a pardon but makes it clear that in doing so he is not exercising the royal prerogative of mercy: the villagers have committed a serious breach of the law (1.2444; see also ll.2016 and 2024) which is to be pardoned only because the judge failed to gather the evidence needed to convict anyone. Legality is thus preserved through the king's use of a legal loophole resulting from the judge's inability to obtain a confession or denunciation

(*29*, p.30). The audience is no doubt intended to admire Fernando's statecraft in pardoning the Maestre and villagers in such a way as to avoid implying that he condones their actions.[71]

Fuenteovejuna illustrates the problems facing those who rule and the qualities which they need in order to govern well and administer justice fairly. It may be, as Carter concludes (*7*, pp.331-32), that Lope's aim was to explore such issues as these, which provide good drama, rather than to advance any specific social or political theory. Macdonald saw the play as an important contribution towards a theory of the state, a message on the duty of governments to ensure that nobody in a position of trust abused his authority (*22*); this may exaggerate the play's political significance, however, for so conventional an idea hardly constitutes a constructive polemical thesis (see Pring-Mill, *2*, p.xxv). According to Javier Herrero, *Fuenteovejuna* celebrates the achievement by the Reyes of a united Catholic Spain, the triumph of the monarchy over a decadent feudalism represented by a corrupt chivalric order eager to extend its territories and temporal power (*13*). This seems plausible, although it does assume in Lope's public a rather detailed knowledge and understanding of what by then were remote events. It might be safer to say that *Fuenteovejuna* simply reflects and supports the patriotic, pious and monarchist sentiments of the age. It is tempting to suppose that in showing a pair of active and decisive sovereigns whose prime concern is for the common good, Lope is implying some criticism of the monarchy of his own time. Such a reading would be supported by the view, still commonly held, that Felipe III was averse to work, lacked initiative, and depended largely on his favourite or *privado*, the Duke of Lerma. Caution, however, is necessary, for as Stradling says of the successors of Felipe II, 'the role in government of the kings themselves is coming to seem considerably greater than earlier writers had supposed...recent detailed studies of Philip III and his son are virtually unanimous

---

[71] Carter suggests (*7*, p.331) that we have 'a hint of the king's expediency' in Fernando's remark (ll.2446-49) that Fuenteovejuna is to remain temporarily in his care: this appears to be a shrewd seizing of a chance to limit the power of the Calatravans, as Lope's audience would perhaps have realized. Eleven years later Fernando was in fact to make himself Grand Master of the Order; Esteban's remark at ll.1628-30 is presumably meant to be prophetic.

in revaluing their administrative abilities'.[72] There is no definite evidence to show that Lope sought to make through *Fuenteovejuna* any kind of challenging or controversial statement about topical national issues.

Love and Harmony

Like many Golden Age *comedias*, *Fuenteovejuna* shows how social order is upset by the forces of evil and finally restored by the forces of good. The play takes for granted the notion of a universal harmony established and sustained by a loving Creator whose design is revealed in the elaborate hierarchy of the great chain of being. The pattern of human society reflects that of the natural order, and the action of the play is a microcosm of the greater conflict between good and evil throughout the universe.

A 'malo cristiano', linked with paganism and the Devil, Fernán Gómez menaces the stability of the nation, the calm of the village and the happiness of Laurencia and Frondoso, whose marriage — a traditional symbol of order and harmony — he interrupts. Throughout the play he inverts or perverts accepted standards and usages: love for him is mere lust, justice becomes injustice, honour is replaced by dishonour; he calls for order while himself planning disruption (ll.1570-71) and complains that order is menaced when people resist him (ll.1044-48 and 1596-1606). At court and in the town moral values are often inverted, but he carries this to an extreme degree.

By contrast, the Reyes and the villagers incarnate order and harmony: Mengo asserts that the universe is a battleground where 'los elementos/ en discordia eterna viven' (ll.373-74) and that this is true also of man, the microcosm, in whom the corresponding humours conflict; Barrildo, however, argues in Platonic and Christian terms that the universe is a place of harmony and love:

> El mundo de acá y de allá,
> Mengo, todo es armonía.
> Armonía es puro amor,
> porque el amor es concierto. (ll.379-82)

Mengo's remark that if the universe is ruled by love, it is by self-

[72] R.A. Stradling, *Europe and the Decline of Spain* (London: George Allen and Unwin, 1981), p.68.

love (ll.383-99) is countered by Barrildo's citing of a sermon he once heard which expounded the concept of an unselfish, spiritual, Platonic love (ll.421-26). Love and order or harmony (the latter often linked with music) are extolled time and again by the villagers: as soon as the action moves to Fuenteovejuna Laurencia and Pascuala identify themselves with true love and marriage as opposed to the lust and libertinage of the Comendador. Describing her orderly daily routine, Laurencia refers to the 'armonía' of the cow frisking in the meadow (l.228), and uses 'concertar' and 'casar' to describe the preparation of the various ingredients which combine to make her meal (ll.229-32). As love between her and Frondoso blossoms, the Comendador receives his first setback in the village at the conclusion to Act I. Here Frondoso's 'Yo me conformo/ con mi estado' (ll.851-52) contrasts with the ambition and self-interest of the Comendador which have led him to rebel against the state, and also with the lust which has caused him to break his vows and pursue women whom, as his vassals, he should honour and protect.

A different kind of love, namely friendship and loyalty towards others, is exemplified by the villagers when they combine to save Frondoso ('amor les ha movido', he tells Fernán Gómez, l.1864), and to give nobody away under torture; Frondoso's love for both Laurencia and his neighbours and friends prevents him from abandoning them when the judge comes to Fuenteovejuna. Mengo comes to display unselfish love for others and is thus reintegrated into the community as it were, joining in the songs which celebrate the lovers' wedding, the defeat of the Comendador and the virtues of the Reyes. Interestingly, his *coplas* on the king and queen express the wish that they may always triumph over dwarves and giants — traditionally the villains of both folktale and chivalric romance, their ill-proportioned bodies suggestive of the disorder that they wreak. Much earlier, in Act I, music and song had linked the villagers with order and harmony when they loyally greeted the Comendador on his return from what they believed was a victory over the infidel. The king and queen, united in their mutual love and shared determination to remedy the 'demasías' of Fernán Gómez (1.709, see also 1.719), are described by Esteban as the defenders of 'nuevas órdenes...con que desórdenes quitan' (ll.1621-22). The expression 'para en uno son' is used of their happy marriage (1.2037) as well as of that of Laurencia and Frondoso (1.1545); order is stressed elsewhere by such words as 'concertaos todos a una' (1.2089) and 'conformes a una' (1.2366) to describe the villagers' united resistance to the judge. Previously the women had set out to attack the Comendador's house 'puestas todas en orden' (1.1829). As Casalduero showed, the conflict between order and disorder is suggested by the frequent juxtaposition of the *redondilla* and *romance* metres (*8*; see Chapter 5, above), and the striking symmetries of the play's structure — a not uncommon feature of the Golden Age *comedia* — also relate to the idea of an essentially ordered reality (see Chapter 3, above).

Fuenteovejuna abounds in examples of how sin (defined by Aquinas as a fall from coherence), disturbs the divinely-established order: objects are misused, moral values are inverted, people are treated as animals, the social fabric is threatened, normally peaceful folk are provoked to destructive violence, women fight like men. As Varey has shown, the play amply illustrates the theme of the world upside down, which has been common in European literature since Classical times. However, in a conclusion which is both reassuring for the audience and satisfying dramatically, the pattern is restored: chaos and confusion are transcended as the Reyes and their loyal subjects meet and the villagers are granted the royal protection which they seek. To quote Varey:

En el *mundo al revés* el orden cósmico, el orden divino, está amenazado, pero siempre al final se restablece la armonía social y vuelve el mundo a sus normas. El tema puede parecer revolucionario, pero básicamente es un reflejo de una sociedad de ideales conservadores. (*36*, p.7)

7 Conclusion

Taking as his starting-point a familiar story, Lope produced in *Fuenteovejuna* a varied, exciting and fast-moving drama in what was probably a short time. Nothing is known of the circumstances of the play's composition but Lope's output was so vast that *Fuenteovejuna* might have been written in a few days;[73] in that case Lope must have had a strong instinctive sense of shape and order, for although it may give an impression of realism and spontaneity, *Fuenteovejuna* is a highly stylized work, abounding in symmetries which reinforce the theme of harmony triumphant. The use of the village community as collective protagonist was an original idea, although the importance of this device ought not to be exaggerated: the main plot turns upon a personal matter, the determination of a resolute young woman to defend her honour against a villainous *hidalgo* and to rescue from his clutches the man she really loves; this is a struggle in which the other villagers gradually become involved. Love is menaced but finally emerges victorious: a common literary situation indeed, but one which is always popular and effective. Other enduring qualities which any audience would find moving and intriguing would include the corruption and redemption of an immature youth, the conversion of a cynic, a nostalgic picture of a simpler and more innocent way of life, and the vindication of the rights of the ordinary citizen, to which is linked the idea of poetic justice. A great deal of the criticism written on *Fuenteovejuna* has been thematic, but Lope was not primarily a moralist who saw in the theatre a convenient vehicle

[73] According to P.E. Russell, Lope 'would have needed to write about twenty-two plays a year to earn even the thousand ducats which made a Castilian farmer of the time think himself well-off. Such amounts were a good deal less than what contemporary English playwrights like Shakespeare expected to get for a play. Poor remuneration must, therefore, be regarded as one reason for the large number of plays written and the need not to spend more than a few days on each' (*Spain: A Companion to Spanish Studies*, ed. P.E. Russell (London: Methuen, 1973), p.353).

for his ideas: it is his skill as a poet and dramatist which distinguishes him. *Fuenteovejuna* impresses as a play full of excitement, humour, pathos, poetry and action, albeit some modern adaptors think otherwise and have made curious modifications as a result.[74]

Although it shows how easily the stability of the state and the happiness of individuals can be menaced by evil, *Fuenteovejuna* is nevertheless reassuring and optimistic in its portrayal of how goodness finally triumphs through the wisdom of rulers and the virtue of their subjects. The play deals with matters of statecraft and the need for those in authority to use their powers well, but the issues at stake are moral rather than political: the villagers turn against the Comendador because he is evil, not because he is an aristocrat and their overlord. Like the basis of the story, the themes in *Fuenteovejuna* are scarcely original: Christian love is shown to be essential both in personal relationships and in affairs of state; evil should be resisted and right and justice defended; every citizen should receive fair and honourable treatment from his rulers. Though presented in what is frequently a vivid and striking manner, these ideas are neither new nor specially controversial; they remain, however, worth stating and defending, whether in Lope's time or in our own.

---

[74] Kirschner mentions versions in which, for instance, Mengo is tortured to death and Jacinta is raped on stage, and in which the King, the Maestre and Manrique are presented as a trio of homosexual lovers. In Fassbinder's version, *Das brennende Dorf*, Fernando denies the villagers a pardon and they turn on him and his followers and kill and eat them in a cannibalistic frenzy. As Kirschner comments, 'al compararse con estas "adaptaciones" contemporáneas, las de los años 30 se quedan pálidas' (*17*, p.264).

Bibliographical Note

A. WORKS BY LOPE

1. *Arte nuevo de hacer comedias en este tiempo*, ed. Federico Sánchez Escribano and Alberto Porqueras Mayo, in *Preceptiva dramática española del Renacimiento y el Barroco* (Madrid: Gredos, 1965), pp.125-36.

2. *Lope de Vega (Five Plays)*, trans. Jill Booty, ed. R.D.F. Pring-Mill (New York: Hill and Wang, Mermaid Dramabooks, 1961). Pring-Mill's valuable introduction considers the background to Lope's plays, the *Arte nuevo* and the underlying principles of Golden Age drama; the short but perceptive section on *Fuenteovejuna* includes a summary of critical approaches to the play up to 1955.

3. *Fuente Ovejuna (dos comedias)*, ed. Francisco López Estrada, Clásicos Castalia, 10 (Madrid: Castalia, 1969). The text of Lope's play is followed by that of Cristóbal de Monroy; there is a good introduction to each play and a concluding comparative study.

4. *Fuente Ovejuna*, ed. Juan María Marín, Letras Hispánicas, 137 (Madrid: Castalia, 1981). Contains a very full introduction which stresses the need to approach the play historically and not to stress its socio-political aspects at the expense of its religious or philosophical elements. Follows 6 in seeing the play as an act of homage to the Duke of Osuna and the Girón family rather than a work exclusively concerned with an episode of social justice.

5. *Fuente Ovejuna*, ed. Maria Grazia Profeti, Hispánicos Universales, 16 (Madrid: Cupsa, 1978). The notes are useful; the long introduction deals mainly with the play's structure.

B. STUDIES

6. Aníbal, C.E., 'The Historical Elements of Lope de Vega's *Fuenteovejuna*', *Publications of the Modern Language Association of America*, 49 (1934), 657-718. A thorough analysis which shows Lope's debt to the chronicle of Rades for both the main plot and the secondary plot of the play; also indicates how Lope departed from his source by making Fernán Gómez the instigator of the capture of Ciudad Real by the Calatravans, a change motivated by a wish to flatter his patron the Duke of Osuna by presenting the Duke's ancestor the Maestre in a more favourable light.

7. Carter, Robin, '*Fuenteovejuna* and Tyranny: Some Problems of Linking Drama with Political Theory', *Forum for Modern Language Studies*, 13 (1977), 313-35. A warning against seeing a play like *Fuenteovejuna* as a vehicle for a specific set of socio-political views which the author is seeking to communicate to his public; suggests that Lope is concerned at least in part with the general difficulty of governing well and the conflict between on the one hand the principles of law and justice and on the other the pressure of circumstance and political necessity. Casts a good deal of light on Act III of the play.

8. Casalduero, Joaquín, '*Fuenteovejuna*', in *Estudios sobre el teatro español* (Madrid: Gredos, 1962), pp.9-44. Originally published in *Revista de Filología Hispánica*, 5 (1943), 21-44. Shows how the *aldea-corte* theme as well as the themes of courtesy and love are reinforced by the play's metrical pattern.

9. Fiore, Robert L., *Drama and Ethos: Natural-Law Ethics in Spanish Golden Age Theater*, Studies in Romance Languages, 14 (Lexington: University Press of Kentucky, 1975). Chapter 2 (pp.14-22) on *Fuenteovejuna* is a revised version of Fiore's 'Natural Law in the Central Ideological Theme of *Fuenteovejuna*', *Hispania* (U.S.A.), 49 (1966), 75-80. Shows how Aristotelian-Thomist concepts of natural law justify the villagers' use of force against a tyrant.

10. Gerli, E. Michael, 'The Hunt of Love: the Literalization of a Metaphor in *Fuenteovejuna*', *Neophilologus*, 63 (1979), 54-58. Shows how the traditional notion of the hunt as an allegory of courtship is seen in the Comendador's pursuit of Laurencia.

11. Gómez-Moriana, A., *Derecho de resistencia y tiranicidio: estudio de una temática en las comedias de Lope de Vega*, Biblioteca Hispánica de Filosofía del Derecho, 1 (Santiago de Compostela: Porto, 1968). Studies Golden Age ideas on tyranny and resistance to tyranny and their possible influence upon plays by Lope in which these issues occur.

12. Hall, J.B., 'Theme and Structure in Lope's *Fuenteovejuna*', *Forum for Modern Language Studies*, 10 (1974), 57-66. Suggests that the rebellion of Fernán Gómez and that of the villagers follow an identical pattern; also shows how careful Lope seems to be in stressing the Comendador's tyrannical behaviour, certain aspects of which may owe something to Aquinas's views on tyranny.

13. Herrero, Javier, 'The New Monarchy: a Structural Reinterpretation of *Fuenteovejuna*', *Revista Hispánica Moderna*, 36 (1970-71), 173-85. An analysis of the play's imagery and of how it illuminates the themes of love triumphant and of the glorification of the Spanish Imperial Monarchy.

14. Hesse, Everett W., 'Los conceptos del amor en *Fuenteovejuna*', *Revista de Archivos, Bibliotecas y Museos*, 75 (1969-72), 305-23. On the various kinds of love — selfish, altruistic, carnal, 'pure', paternal, etc. — presented in the play.

15. Kirschner, Teresa J., *El protagonista colectivo en 'Fuenteovejuna'*,
     Studia Philologica Salmanticensia, Anejos: Estudios, 1 (Salamanca:
     Ediciones Universidad de Salamanca, 1979). An interesting study of the
     'pueblo-masa' as a character; also examines Lope's treatment of his
     source-material. Useful information on translations and adaptations of
     the play and on the various approaches to it taken by twentieth-century
     critics (see also *17* and *16*, respectively; though published earlier, these
     contain more up-to-date information, for the bibliography of *15* stops at
     1971).

16. ——, 'Evolución de la crítica de *Fuenteovejuna*, de Lope de Vega, en el
     siglo XX', *Cuadernos Hispanoamericanos*, nos 320-21 (1977), 450-65.

17. ——, 'Sobrevivencia de una comedia: historia de la difusión de
     Fuenteovejuna', *Revista Canadiense de Estudios Hispánicos*, 1
     (1976-77), 255-71.

18. Larson, Donald R., *The Honor Plays of Lope de Vega* (Cambridge,
     Mass.: Harvard University Press, 1977). Has a sensible study of
     Fuenteovejuna (pp.82-112).

19. López Estrada, Francisco, 'La canción "Al val de Fuente Ovejuna" de
     la comedia *Fuente Ovejuna* de Lope', in *Homenaje a William L.
     Fichter: estudios y ensayos sobre el teatro antiguo hispánico, y otros
     ensayos*, ed. A. David Kossoff and José Amor y Vázquez (Madrid:
     Castalia, 1971), pp.453-68. A study of the content, style and dramatic
     function of the song performed at the wedding of Laurencia and
     Frondoso.

20. ——, '*Fuente Ovejuna* en el teatro de Lope y de Monroy (Consideración
     crítica de ambas obras)', *Anales de la Universidad Hispalense*, 26 (1965),
     1-91.

21. ——, 'Los villanos filosóficos y políticos (La configuración de *Fuente
     Ovejuna* a través de los nombres y "apellidos")', *Cuadernos
     Hispanoamericanos*, nos 238-40 (1969), 518-42. Good on the influence
     of pastoral literature upon the names of certain characters, the lifestyle
     of the villagers and their ideas on love.

22. Macdonald, Inez I., 'An Interpretation of *Fuente Ovejuna*', *Babel*, 1
     (1940), 51-62. Examines the themes of *cortesía* and love. Sees the play as
     concerned with political theory and the duty of governments to ensure
     that those in authority do not exceed their powers.

23. Marín, Diego, *La intriga secundaria en el teatro de Lope de Vega*,
     Colección Studium, 22 (Toronto: University of Toronto Press; Mexico
     City: Andrea, 1958). Stresses the thematic and structural importance of
     the sub-plot: it shows the *hubris* of Fernán Gómez on a national and
     political level, complementing the main plot which shows it on a moral
     and social level (pp.58-64).

24. ——, *Uso y función de la versificación dramática en Lope de Vega*, 2nd
     ed., Estudios de Hispanófila, 2 (Valencia: Castalia, 1968). Has few
     specific references to *Fuenteovejuna*, but the conclusions on Lope's use

of different metres in other works throw some light on his technique in this play.

25. McCrary, William C., '*Fuenteovejuna*: its Platonic Vision and Execution', *Studies in Philology*, 58 (1961), 179-92. Argues that the play is essentially about the triumph of order over chaos and the restoration of a threatened harmony, pointing to the start of a new order for the whole of Spain.

26. Menéndez Pelayo, Marcelino, *Estudios sobre el teatro de Lope de Vega* (Santander: CSIC, 1949), V, 171-82. Reproduces Rades's account of the village uprising and indicates Lope's debt to it; sees the play as pro-monarchic but at the same time having democratic and even anarchic implications. This study first appeared as a prologue to *Fuenteovejuna* in the 1899 Spanish Academy edition of Lope's works.

27. Moir, Duncan W., 'Lope de Vega's *Fuenteovejuna* and the *Emblemas morales* of Sebastián de Covarrubias Horozco (with a few remarks on *El villano en su rincón*)', in *Homenaje a William L. Fichter* (see *19*), pp.537-46. Points out that Covarrubias's book has an emblem on the Fuenteovejuna affair and suggests that this may have given Lope the idea for his play.

28. Parker, A.A., 'Reflections on a new definition of "Baroque" Drama', *Bulletin of Hispanic Studies*, 30 (1953), 142-51. Includes a discussion of *Fuenteovejuna* which maintains that the play has thematic unity but not (at least until the end of Act II) unity of action.

29. Pring-Mill, R.D.F., 'Sententiousness in *Fuente Ovejuna*', *Tulane Drama Review*, 7 (1962), 5-37. Examines the significance of the numerous proverbs and general moralizing remarks in the play, which is seen as basically Platonic: behind particular situations can be glimpsed universal principles.

30. Ramírez de Arellano, Rafael, 'Rebelión de Fuente Obejuna contra el Comendador Mayor de Calatrava Fernán Gómez de Guzmán (1476)', *Boletín de la Real Academia de la Historia*, 39 (1901), 446-512. Suggests, after a study of documents in the Ayuntamiento of Córdoba, that the rebellion of Fuenteovejuna was stirred up by the citizens of Córdoba who hoped thereby to limit the influence of the Order of Calatrava.

31. Ribbans, G.W., 'The Meaning and Structure of Lope's *Fuenteovejuna*', *Bulletin of Hispanic Studies*, 31 (1954), 150-170. Sees the play as loosely constructed but unified thematically; *Fuenteovejuna* deals with the relationship of the various elements in society, a relationship which is disturbed and then finally restored. Spanish translation in *El teatro de Lope de Vega: artículos y estudios*, ed. José Francisco Gatti (Buenos Aires: Editorial Universitaria de Buenos Aires, 1962, repr. 1967), pp.91-123.

32. Salomon, Noël, *Recherches sur le thème paysan dans la 'comedia' au temps de Lope de Vega*, Bibliothèque des Hautes Études Hispaniques,

31 (Bordeaux: Féret et Fils, 1965). Contains a number of illuminating references to *Fuenteovejuna*, especially with regard to honour and to the noble-peasant conflict. Sees the play as being feudal in spirit and yet anti-feudal in its implications.

33. Serrano, Carlos, 'Métaphore et idéologie: sur le tyran de *Fuenteovejuna* de Lope de Vega', *Les Langues Néo-Latines*, 4 (1971), 31-53. Claims that the play, through the 'anachronistic' figure of Fernán Gómez, signifies the problems of early seventeenth-century Spain, a society in which 'the tyrannical demons of a feudal past had yet to be exorcised'.

34. Soons, C. Alan, 'Two historical Comedias and the Question of *Manierismo*', *Romanische Forschungen*, 73 (1961), 339-46. On the theme of order and harmony.

35. Spitzer, Leo, 'A Central Theme and its Structural Equivalent in Lope's *Fuenteovejuna*', *Hispanic Review*, 23 (1955), 274-92. Examines the theme of Platonic harmony which is presented in musical terms: the play is a kind of opera, reflecting a simple dream of universal Christian harmony. Like *31*, reproduced in Gatti's *El teatro de Lope de Vega* (pp.124-47).

36. Varey, J.E., *La inversión de valores en "Fuenteovejuna"*, Lectiones, 5 (Santander: Universidad Internacional Menéndez Pelayo, 1976). A study of the theme of 'the world upside down' as it appears in *Fuenteovejuna*.

37. Wardropper, Bruce W., '*Fuente Ovejuna*: *el gusto* and *lo justo*', *Studies in Philology*, 53 (1956), 159-71. Sees the play as concerned with an examination of human behaviour rather than with political issues. The central theme is love, a quality necessary for good relations between individuals and between groups; ethics and politics are really inseparable.

38. Wilson, Edward M., and Duncan Moir, *The Golden Age: Drama 1492-1700* (London: Ernest Benn; New York: Barnes and Noble, 1971). A volume in *A Literary History of Spain*, ed. R.O. Jones. The chapter on Lope, by Moir, has a useful section on *Fuenteovejuna* (pp.61-66) which is especially good on the question of honour as a dramatic theme and in society.

39. Young, Richard A., *La figura del Rey y la institución real en la comedia lopesca* (Madrid: José Porrúa Turanzas, 1979). Makes interesting points on the presentation of monarchs in Lope's drama; a few references specifically to *Fuenteovejuna*.

CRITICAL GUIDES TO SPANISH TEXTS

Edited by
J.E. Varey and A.D. Deyermond